What Others are Saying About

PRIME TIME DADS:
45 Reasons to Embrace Midlife Fatherhood

Larry King, CNN broadcast legend:
"The best thing that ever happened to me in life is being able to be a later in life dad. I'm 79 years old, I have three grown children, and the lights of my life are my preteen boys. Later life fatherhood keeps me young, keeps me vital, and makes me feel relevant each and every day. I urge you to read *PRIME TIME DADS*. Its point of view is young and vital and relevant each and every page."

Adriana Trigiani, best-selling author:
"Len Filppu has written a hilarious, heartfelt, and fresh take on midlife fatherhood in *PRIME TIME DADS*. This is a superb how-to manual for parents everywhere. It's also the perfect gift for the man in your life. Brimming with common sense and filled with helpful hints, it's a celebration of fatherhood written by a dad who clearly loves every moment of it. A home run!"

David Carnoy, CNET executive editor and co-author of *Fathers of a Certain Age: the Joys and Problems of Middle-Aged Fatherhood*:
"*PRIME TIME DADS* takes a fun, optimistic look at what it's like to be an 'older' father. While this book is geared toward men aged around 40 or so, women who are involved with so-called 'reluctant dads' would be wise to leave it out in a conspicuous place where it might be easily discovered."

Kristi Walsh, Ph.D., psychoanalyst, marriage and family therapist:
"As a mental health professional of 30 years, I strongly support the notion of mid-life parenting. An individual's ability to self-reflect with honesty, to move past one's ego and genuinely love another, and the generativity that compels one to invest in the next generation – these are the developmental achievements of mid-life and the parental qualities children need.

I am infinitely grateful for my husband, a prime time dad, who brought the emotional maturity and groundedness, patience, and humor that helped bond us as a family when we adopted our son at age 3. My husband just turned 60 and we are pursuing another adoption!"

David Zeiger, filmmaker, Displaced Films:
"Len Filppu has grabbed onto a profound truth and treated it with the humor it deserves. My own 'bonus round' with my two daughters, starting in my mid-40s, has been filled with such boundless joy that I could not possibly imagine my life without them. Len has captured the fun and heartache, the craziness and gratitude of these wonderful years. And best of all, it comes from his own head, heart, and spitup-stained shirts. *PRIME TIME DADS* is a joy to read."

Tom Parker, *New York Times* best-selling author:
"As an older dad myself, I found *PRIME TIME DADS* entertaining, instructive, heart-warming, funny and true. I liked the style, tone and sentiment. The writing, too. The writing, especially."

Frank LaLoggia, film director, *Lady in White*, composer/screenwriter:
"Len Filppu once again proves that he is the Jean Shepherd of our times: funny, insightful and human!"

PRIME TIME DADS

45 REASONS TO EMBRACE MIDLIFE FATHERHOOD

LEN FILPPU

Bright Lights Press
PALO ALTO, CALIFORNIA

Bright Lights Press
P.O. Box 306
Palo Alto, CA 94303
www.BrightLightsPress.com

Book Layout @2013 BookDesignTemplates.com

PRIME TIME DADS: 45 Reasons to Embrace Midlife Fatherhood / Len Filppu. -- 1st ed.
ISBN: 978-1-939555-08-3 paperback

With lifelong love to my courageous wife, Lucy,
my confident son, and my dazzling daughter.
Remember, we can find a solution to any problem.

TABLE OF CONTENTS

....

Introduction   1

45 Reasons to Embrace Midlife Fatherhood

Section I. At the Starting Line

1   Today's 50 is Yesterday's 40, or Less   15
2   You Already Got Your Ya-Yas Out!   19
3   It's Quality, not Quantity, of Time with
     Your Children   23
4   Your Money and Business Affairs are
     In Better Shape   27
5   Don't Retire to a Rocker, Keep on Rockin'   33
6   You're Wiser and Ready for the Emotional
     Turbulence of Fatherhood   37
7   Enjoy Great Sex During Ovulation Orgies   42
8   Behold Your Radiant Pregnant Wife   45
9   You're Now Less Self-Centered, More
     Ready to Give Back   47
10   Say So Long to Loneliness   51
11   Old Dogs Can Learn New Tricks   55

Section II. Off and Running

12   Never Again Be Bored   63
13   Transform Fledgling Wrinkles Into
     Laugh Lines   68
14   You Can Spend More Time with the Kids
     in Their Formative Years   74
15   Fight Alzheimer's Disease?   78
16   There's Lots More Help Out There Now   82
17   Sex in Your First Year of Fatherhood   86
18   Hang Out with a Younger Crowd   87
19   Finally Get Your Home Theater Cranking 91
20   You're Old Enough to Act Like a Child   96
21   Fulfill Your Need for More Meaning
     in Life   100

Section III. Establishing a Rhythm

22   You Have More Patience and Empathy   109
23   Change Past Times to First Times   113
24   You're Now a More Wily Coyote   118
25   You're Primed for a Primal Adventure   122
26   Find a New World of Art   126
27   Holiday Routine Comes Alive   133
28   You're a Better Multi-Tasking Problem
     Solver   140

29 Rediscover Your Parents   144
30 You Know Yourself Better   153
31 Create a New Family History with
    New Memories   157
32 You Can Still Become a Hero   163

Section IV. Savoring the Burn
33 Fatherhood's a Great Reason to Stay
    in Shape   169
34 Coach Your Favorite Sport(s)   174
35 You've Overcome Most of Your Bad
    Habits   181
36 Your Rut is Already Fully Decorated   186
37 You Now Care Even Less About What
    Others Think   191

Section V. In the Zone
38 Reintroduce Yourself to Yourself   197
39 Truly Expand Your Consciousness   205
40 Discover Your Parallel Universe   207
41 Slow Down the Acceleration of Time   210
42 You'll Stay Married and Live Longer   214

Section VI. Pushing Forward the Finish Line

43 Having Kids Will Keep You Young   221
44 Join the World's Largest Fraternity   225
45 There's a Profound Need for Fathers   229

Concluding Remarks   233

Acknowledgments   235

About the Author   237

INTRODUCTION

....

When faced with first time fatherhood at the age of 49, I didn't know whether to celebrate with champagne... or hemlock. The news was a surprise, like an unexpected slap across the face (yes, I've earned a few of those), and my immediate reaction was fear, a primal, mind-racing, where'd-I-lose-my-wallet peaking-panic fear.

Would I have enough energy for fatherhood? How in the world could I give up my leisurely latte freedom for dirty diapers? Would I live long enough to make a proper go of it? Would younger parents mistake me for grandpa? Would I sit on bleachers at little league games dozing and drooling and dreaming of Woodstock?

As it's turned out, those fears proved to be the unfounded, paranoid phantoms of a mind skewed by our society's irrational rush to celebrate youth over wisdom. What I discovered through midlife fatherhood was a deeper, richer reality lived daily at a profoundly more exciting and satisfying level.

Midlife is Prime Time for Fatherhood

I found out that my 40s and 50s were actually my best time, in fact my prime time, to appreciate and accept my role as a new father. These are my prime years, when I'm emotionally mature enough to handle parenthood's dogging demands, wise enough to find deeper meaning and humor amidst the chaotic kid circus, and crafty enough to scheme and deal from the bottom of the deck if and when necessary.

Whether we call it midlife, later-in-life, mature, late blooming, or just plain wacky fatherhood, prime time was the perfect time for me to focus – unencumbered by youthful passions and demands– on being the best dad I could be.

And the benefits of becoming a dad a bit later in life came as such a surprise to me that I wanted to climb the highest hill and shout out my euphoric eureka for other men and women to hear. *PRIME TIME DADS: 45 Reasons to Embrace Midlife Fatherhood* is the result.

I've been tested and challenged with regularity over the last 13 years of fatherhood, and for the most part, I've surprised myself by rising to the occasions. By becoming a prime time dad, I discovered a more authentic, more talented, multifaceted, and interesting me, and I opened the door to the most exciting years of my life.

A Bit of Background

I was previously married without children and divorced. My current wife, Lucy, was aged 36 when we learned of our pregnancy in 1999. We hadn't planned for a family, mostly used birth control, and news of the gestation manifestation came as a complete surprise.

Living and working in northern California's high tech Silicon Valley, I was accustomed to my freedoms, enjoyed my lack of familial responsibilities, and relished my ability to spontaneously pick up and go to Starbucks or Aruba or chill in my man cave listening to the entire Beatles Anthology just about any time I so desired.

I'd always wanted a family and figured it would all fall into place someday, but as the years went by and my relationships did not mix up the right magic, I'd settled into a mellow mindset in which kids were great but it seemed the universe had ordained them to populate other people's lives.

But lightning struck. That fickle universe dialed my number. We had a choice, and we chose to make a family. We now have a 13-year-old son and a 10-year-old daughter who share our genes and dreams. Even at the late-blooming age of 49, becoming a father was the best choice I ever made.

Turning the Paradigm Upside Down

Society subtly programs us to think and act in certain ways, but paths are winding and wanderers vary. It's often the challenge to orthodoxy and new ways of looking at familiar paradigms that make the exploration interesting.

That's the way fatherhood worked for me. Sure, I knew what the "proper" program was, that I was supposed to get married and have children in my earlier years, work hard to make enough money to raise them, and then enjoy myself in my later years of retirement in an empty nest.

But I enjoyed myself in my earlier years. A lot. I lived and worked adventurously, traveled, partied, and did many of the things I imagine people who have children early on long to do but postpone because of their familial responsibilities. And I had an empty nest for three decades. I now enjoy having a full house, and I'm looking forward to a future filled with close body contact.

Please don't get me wrong. I'm not advocating that all men should wait until their 40s to have children. I know that most prime time dads are fathers of second families, and that biology works differently for men than it does for women.

But I'd drifted so far off the traditional path of fatherhood that I figured it was no longer a viable option, and then when it suddenly became a living, breathing, eating, excreting reality, I figured it was the curse and burden and penance I had to pay for living my particular brand of freestyle life on this planet.

Vast Reservoir of Talents

But I was joyfully wrong. I discovered that I, and most mature men in their prime, have an enormous reservoir of unique skills, talents, and life experiences that can be tapped to help us not just survive but thrive as great fathers.

The experience, knowledge and wisdom of men in midlife supply an abundance of specific tools that can be used to build a solid fatherhood foundation, framework, and future. To me, prime time fatherhood is not an issue of being better late than never. It's an issue of actually being *better later.*

Ladies, Listen Up!

Attention women with a prime time, mature or late-blooming husband, boyfriend, son, grandson, nephew, colleague, buddy, bodyguard or boy toy who you think might make a great dad.

While PRIME TIME DADS is written by a man for men from a male point of view, I'm acutely aware that the majority of men probably won't buy a book like this, let alone read it, without your help.

So it's up to you ladies out there to read and laugh with it, think about the messages behind the madcap, and then give it to the prime time men in your lives who may need an encouraging, sly and wry shoehorn to facilitate their reluctant steps into the big boots of fatherhood.

Stuff this book into his golf or bowling bag, place it by his toilet throne, tell him it's nighttime reading before afternoon delight. I don't know, hide it in the sports pages or wrap it up in fried bacon, but get him to look at it.

Use PRIME TIME DADS as a "rattle prod" to shock your routine-rutted bull into considering new pastures. This book just might change his attitude about fatherhood, and change his life, and yours, for the better.

What is Midlife?

For the purposes of this book, prime time midlife for a man is somewhere between the ages of 40 and 60 or so. And while many of the reasons to embrace fatherhood discussed in this book can apply to men of any age, they all made a distinct impression on my over-40, but most certainly not over-the-hill, brain.

Now, many of you ladies out there reading this who've witnessed how we men behave at football games, or fuel up at all-you-can-eat buffets, or noticed how our focus instinctively shifts from the menu to the waitress's décolletage, may be asking yourselves, "You call that a mature man?"

Some men mature earlier, some not at all. My contention is that most men who've approached or moved beyond the age of 40 will relate to the observations in *PRIME TIME DADS.*

But again, this book is for everyone, any age, men and women alike, who are considering parenthood, who are parents, or who were of parents born.

Truth, Not Youth-Obsessed

I was truly intimidated by the prospect of later blooming fatherhood, yet discovered it was the best thing I ever did. This book presents an important, alternative point of view, almost entirely neglected in our youth-obsessed culture. This message deserves to be heard and considered.

The issue of midlife fatherhood is particularly pertinent today as U.S. life expectancies rise, as women who have postponed motherhood due to career or relationship decisions hear louder the ticking of biology's clock, and those who for health or other reasons may now be considering adoption a bit later in their lives. And as our country's divorce rate remains high, many men face the prospect of prime time fatherhood within a second marriage or blended family.

We're so brainwashingly bombarded by images of "perfect" parents in their 20s, that it's only right and fair play that mature men (and especially the millions of women who love them and may wish to encourage them to envision the rewards of fatherhood) get a real life view of midlife fatherhood.

What this Book is About

This is not a scholastic book of sociology or psychology or a how-to book of proper parental advice. It is not a book filled with the latest research and census data.

It is a series of unabashedly optimistic, hopefully humorous, stereotype-smashing, personal point-of-view essays from my heart. The material is based upon my own real life experiences, offbeat observations, and Visine-eyed views from the foxhole of prime time fatherhood. I figure there must be others out there to hear, appreciate and maybe even benefit from my story.

This book is intended to give men who are in their prime years a laugh or two, something to think about, and a positive, encouraging look at how their life experiences provide them with abundant critical skills they can employ to excel in their role as a prime time dad.

It explores advantages we older guys have over younger men on this crazy, exciting journey of fatherhood.

It's the Run, Not the Race

I enjoy a 10K run as a healthful exercise, a pursuit of personal goals, and a shared social event, not primarily as a competitive race. The training process, pre-run excitement, body and esteem benefits, camaraderie, new scenery, and pasta loading are more important to me than the finish line results.

This book's "45 Reasons" are divided into loosely chronological sections— At the Starting Line, Off and Running, Establishing a Rhythm, Savoring the Burn, In the Zone, and Pushing Forward the Finish Line— that underscore the philosophical notion that it's the overall journey of midlife fatherhood that really matters, not any preconceived destination.

Required Disclaimer

Not every man who can grow hair more effectively from his ears than on his scalp should become a father. Parenthood is serious business, and the world already has enough part-time parents and delinquent dads. But men who are sincere about considering the awe-inspiring responsibilities and rewards of midlife fatherhood will find encouragement in *PRIME TIME DADS*.

From the Heart

I've been called many things in my life, but the only name that magically transforms the chemistry of my soul is "Dad." That word, when I stop to really hear it, uttered by my children in myriad ways and with increasing skill and strategy, melts me with a unique and profound love never felt as a childless man. It fills me with the courage and energy to soldier on, and viscerally connects me to my own past, our shared futures, and a universal human condition.

Here's to all the prime time men who may be uncertain about becoming a father, who think they may not have the energy, who lack the confidence to go for it, or remain reluctant to take on the enormous responsibilities. It's also for all the women who love them: the wives, partners, girlfriends, single moms, sisters, mothers, aunts, grannies, colleagues and friends.

Whether through adoption, second marriages, blended families, medical advances, social volunteerism or the old-fashioned way, prime time fatherhood is a growing trend worth exploring. The process has profoundly transformed me into a better human being. It's turned out to be the challenge of a lifetime, and the very making of my life.

I sincerely wish all of you good luck, health, and joy on your journey. And I hope you greyer guys with an inkling you may love fatherhood get to experience the down-to-the-molecule metamorphosis induced by fledgling voices mouthing, "Hey, Dad!"

Len Filppu

Section I.

At the Starting Line

ONE

....

TODAY'S 50 IS
YESTERDAY'S 40, OR
LESS

At the start of the 20th century, the average American lived only 47 years. Life expectancy for that same American born today is approximately 78 years. Life expectancy in the United States is currently longer than ever before, and it is on the increase.

These advances are not driven by chugging Methuselah mash from the latest fountain of youth or even esoteric medical innovations affordable mainly by billionaires. It's about down to earth basics that are directly within our control.

If we take care of ourselves, eat wisely, get exercise, go for regular medical and dental exams, and avoid hazardous activities such as smoking and discussing politics with irrational relatives, we can stay healthy, active and vital well into our later decades.

In fact, new research from the Max Planck Institute for Demographic Research in Rostock, Germany, was recently heralded with large font headlines proclaiming, "72 is the new 30!" The research shows that human life expectancy is rising faster than it has for 200 millennia. Primitive hunter gatherers, at age 30, had the same odds of dying as a modern Swedish or Japanese man would face at age 72.

Gains in human longevity are not attributed to genetics but to the invention of antibiotics and vaccines, improvements in agricultural efficiency, and the greater availability of food and clean water.

It's confirming what we already know. We get a better shot at living longer if we change our behaviors. Remember what Mama told and scolded. No nicotine, limit the booze, get outdoors and get some exercise, go to bed at a reasonable hour, eat your vegetables, and don't be a stranger at the doctor's office.

Men today are not content to be saddled with addled characterizations of male maturation drawn not from reality but from cartoonish, buffoonish television sitcoms. Those obsolete notions about middle-aged men flopping onto sofas to fall comatose watching Matlock reruns are outdated, out of line, and just plain out to lunch.

The forward march of health, medicine, and technology provides everyone with virtually limitless opportunities for renewal, redefinition, and revitalization. Better medicine, nutrition, and physical and psychological activities are widely available to a maturing population that refuses to fade quietly away and continues to challenge and demand more from existing systems.

Midlife years are becoming an active and even perfect prime time for creative changes, for making unfulfilled dreams come true, for re-evaluating and attaining deeper meaning in life. Mature people are increasingly devising new strategies to stay active, healthy, vibrant, involved, and aware throughout their years.

Do not accept the moldy oldy stereotypes. Smash the mold. You're as young as you think, and when you think about it, you're still a work in progress. Every day forward gives you another shot at retooling your conduct, redefining your potential, reimagining your future, and recharging your spirit.

Apply a healthy dose of skepticism to being told you're too old for fatherhood. I was so bombarded and brainwashed by Madison Avenue and fractured folk tales telling me only youth should have youngsters that I almost missed the single most rewarding journey of my life.

TWO

....

YOU ALREADY GOT
YOUR YA-YAS OUT

Kids thrive in a stable, predictable, safe world of order, love, and boundaries. As a more mature midlife male, you are most likely now infinitely more capable of providing such an environment. Why? Because you've probably already acted out and grown past most of your wild rascal shenanigans.

You've no doubt traveled around, played around, dabbled around, and wandered around the block a few times. And since you've already been there and done that, the gnawing sense that you might be missing that irresistible yet elusive "something" out there has diminished.

Your insane itching urge to shuck it all to pursue your individual forms of madness is now a more dormant desire, most likely fueling fond memories instead of immature action.

Hey, I've been to the rodeo a few times, and I've roared and been gored. But the best thing I ever did during my sowing of wild oats days was very purposefully not become a parent. Somehow, I knew better.

Hitchhiking around the states, living in a commune, sleeping on couches throughout the country on a presidential campaign, and helping make a low-budget, B-movie horror film were just not conducive to a stable relationship with a spouse or children.

How shall I put this? When I was young, eager for experience, knew I'd live forever, and the rules applied to everyone else but me, I would go and flow wherever the action seemed most intriguing.

Back in those days, especially my 20s and 30s, nothing could stand in the way of me doing what I wanted. If I'd had a family during those times of intense personal exploration, I surely would've been a neglectful father.

A family at that time would have prevented me from trying my hand at free-wheeling investigations of travel, politics, and film. I would have felt imprisoned. I would've been pacing the baby's room, blaming my wife and kids for my confinement, growing resentful, then bitter, longing for what I missed, and planning my escapes.

As a prime time dad who's lived out those dreams (with nightmares), I'm now ready for the more cozy confines of the parental penitentiary. Heck, instead of trying to tunnel out of the place, I've helped reproduce more inmates to join me on the inside. I'm not imprisoned by my children, I'm impassioned.

You see, I've had enough dates, lost enough money in Vegas, scuba-ed in Aruba, partied hearty, emerged through plenty of scrapes and traps, and have now matured enough to realize I don't need nor want to revisit any of it. Enough is enough. If you're a more mature guy, you know what I mean.

I thank my lucky stars that I survived my past, lived hard to realize some of my dreams, and that I don't have to do it all again. I'm now ready to embrace wholeheartedly my family life.

I already got my ya-yas out. I'm now level-headedly ready and eager for this new adventure. And you know what? As it's turning out, raising kids is truly the wildest trip of all. They're born

with an endless supply of ya-yas. That ironic kar-
mic wheel simply creaked full circle.

THREE

··

IT'S QUALITY, NOT QUANTITY, OF TIME WITH YOUR CHILDREN

Sure, statistically speaking, midlife men may have a bit less time left to wander this planet than younger men, but that end-game knowledge will actually help make life with your children more conscious, mindful, and special.

You'll not be mesmerized by the illusion that you have forever. You'll tend to make each day with your kids really count. You won't answer "Next week," to every request to build a fort in the living room, or bat balloons, or ride the tricycle, or deal another hand of "Fish."

You'll savor your time with your kids, and your parental enjoyment and their emotional development will flourish accordingly. Because you are acutely aware that time is limited, you'll be more apt to enrich the years you have by loving, connecting, teaching, and sharing deeply, moment by precious afforded moment.

Of course, no one can keep up a trance-like state of pure poetic parenting. But I believe the prime time dad has the necessary time under his belt to understand that time with kids is a quality, not quantity, issue.

Look at all the examples of children who've lived years and years with indifferent, uninvolved parents. The trashy tell-all books of these resentful rascals are a mainstay of popular publishing. As a prime time father, you may still star in such livid pages, but you have the proper philosophical bent that can lead to the development of a true, tight paternal connection.

As a later blooming dad, I understand the chances are that I may not be around long into my children's adult lives. And this is very the reason I decided to spend more time with them when they are youngsters. I rearranged my work life, focused on consulting and my long suppressed writing dreams, and became a deeply involved dad.

If I wasn't going to be around when they were 50, I sure as taxes was going to be around when they were five!

I've always figured that my quality time with them in their early lives would bolster and nourish them later on. I believe this is true, and it was verified to me recently by a friend.

When growing up, her dad was older than those of most of her friends' dads. But he spent a great deal of quality time with her throughout her childhood. He demonstrably enjoyed being with her, participated in her interests and life, and showed his love for her through emotion and deed.

She told me that when he died, she was shaken to her core. But deep within her grief, she realized that her dad had spent so much time with her because he loved her dearly. His attention proved she was worthy of love. This epiphany sustained her during her loss and still supports her during rough patches today, decades later.

Prime time dads know time is limited, and therefore are perfectly suited to dive right in to create the quality times and bonds with their children that will live with and nurture them forever.

Close, heartfelt connections with my children are loving, life-enhancing legacies. And the crazy thing I realized as a later in life dad is, they're so much fun to create!

··

FOUR

YOUR MONEY AND BUSINESS AFFAIRS ARE IN BETTER SHAPE

I'm not suggesting all you midlife guys are picking up the tab after lunching with Warren Buffet and Carlos Slim. The truth is, it was not so long ago that I struggled to feed 50 pennies into enough of those paper coin tubes from the bank to buy a dozen eggs to spread over toasted stale bread for a week's worth of meals.

But over the years, you've probably learned not to buy any bridges (whatever the discounted price), how to shop around for low interest rates, and how to wiggle and wrangle within a tight budget when necessary.

You've learned the wisdom of having an emergency cash fund, regular investments into a retirement account, and chances are you have a bit more money than you did when you were starting out.

That's as good as gold, because lack of money is one of the single greatest causes of familial stress and divorce, toxic conditions for parents and children alike.

Having a bit of a cash cushion really helps when it comes to parenthood because you'll need lots of new stuff and breaks from the infinite list of new duties that expend finite amounts of energy.

It will be most advantageous to you, your spouse, and your children if you can afford some of the basics and some simple luxuries that can help you stay focused and fresh for your child rearing activities.

I'm not going to kid around as you consider kids around. The bills add up. There are expenses everywhere you turn, including cribs, diaper stations, rockers, strollers, baby clothes, play toys, car seats, and all kinds of things you've probably never thought of and wouldn't think of unless you were suddenly doing all that is humanly possible to do the best you can for your own children.

And as you keep feeding those tender tots, they'll get older and craftier, their tastes will change, and the toys they consume will transform into expensive electronics. They'll soon start lobbying for their own cell phones, concert tickets, and vacations in Hawaii, and you'll be moving fast toward car and college costs.

My wife and I gratefully discovered that the world of parenting is filled with folks who care and share. We were given many hand-me-down items and clothing, and in the same vein, we still give decent used items to friends. We shared and compared and bought much used and second-hand. And we didn't buy everything the deviously savvy marketers tried to sell us.

Groucho Marx is credited with saying, "Money frees you from doing things you dislike. Since I dislike doing nearly everything, money is handy." Money is indeed handy, and since you'll be busy juggling many new (and thrilling) parenting activities, a few extra bucks to throw at a handy man, a mow-blow-and-go gardener, someone to shovel the driveway, or a maid service to clean the house on occasion will make you grin like Groucho.

And don't forget the babysitter. You and your spouse will need some time off together, sans children, to decompress, center yourselves, and discuss all the things you haven't accomplished as parents.

Please do not misunderstand me. You need not be rich to raise children. But the prime time dad, who probably has a fatter wallet to match his expanding waistline, can apply those resources in positive ways that enhance the child rearing process for all concerned.

And now a word or two about business affairs. "Be prepared" is good advice when it comes to business and legal affairs, and since I'm older and therefore have heard it repeated more often, maybe it's actually sunk into my grey matter a bit deeper.

If you're considering siring youngsters, having your business affairs in order is a distinct plus. Middle-aged guys are more apt to have life and health insurance policies paid up, wills and trusts drawn and signed, deeds sitting in safe deposit boxes, retirement funds maturing, employment contracts in effect, and the like.

Even if you're like I was pre-fatherhood, that is, not fully on top of my business affairs, consider it a perfect motivating time to get on the ball and put things right.

For years, I ignored my investments, simply selecting boxes with hot sounding mutual funds on company 401(k) forms in which to place savings, hoping for increases but not really knowing what I was doing.

Becoming a dad made me reassess my lax attitude toward investing. So, I began to research the murky world of investing. I found the process of learning about investing fun and empowering. No longer was I merely handing over my savings to someone else to control. I began to manage much of it, and have saved on commissions with a basic no-load, low cost, index mutual funds approach.

My point here is not that I'm day trading esoteric derivatives. It's that becoming a dad prodded me to get a better handle on important business matters, and we as a family are much better off as a result.

The prime time aged man usually has more of his act together in the cloudy grey areas of the dismal science, and this adds up to a brighter more secure environment in which to raise a family.

When the offspring circus explodes in your living room, you'll appreciate that bedrock security, because as with almost everything else in your new parental role, you'll be working without a net.

Please Note: If any of you are considering having children in order to benefit from the many available (but always changing) income tax deductions, college savings plans, gifts to minors advantages, and the like, my advice is that you do the world a favor and make an appointment for a vasectomy. Cut a bit more than just your taxes.

FIVE

....

DON'T RETIRE TO A ROCKER, KEEP ON ROCKIN'

Prime time dads may reach retirement age sooner than younger fathers, but in no way am I daydreaming about vegetating on some front porch rocking chair wearing a stained tie, worn slippers, and a feeble smile like some latter day version of Ward Cleaver on a Valium drip. I'll bet you aren't, either.

I'm part of that baby-boomer subset who resided for several years in The Woodstock Nation (I now lean toward the Colbert Nation). Back in the headshop daze of those turbulent days, so many young people were dying at age 27, notably the Forever 27 Club of Jimi Hendrix, Janis Joplin, and

Jim Morrison, that even age 30 seemed old. Trust me on that, even though I'm over 30.

But take a fresh look at *Rolling Stone* magazine, which is still crazy (and relevant) after all these years. 60- and 70-year-old rockers still fill concert stadiums, and attract the attention of younger fans, popular media, and groping groupies.

While not everyone can afford the lavish luxury, the green M&Ms, or the blood transfusions of the rock star lifestyle, what continues to amaze me is that these old war horses just keep on trucking. The limits of what is possible and what is acceptable later in life keep getting pushed forward, to new horizons, kinda out of sight, man.

As a prime time dad, I'll be smack dab in an active phase of parenthood during what might be considered traditional retirement years. Okay, bring it on. I'm looking forward to it. I don't want to retire to an empty nest with little to do and faded dreams. I'm looking forward to a bustling nest, with plenty to do in my faded jeans.

While I wisely evaded and ignored the baby roller coaster as it whizzed by in my freedom-loving, lava lamp, hitchhiking days, becoming a midlife dad is making the dormant dream come true.

Better late than never, and later has never been better than it is right now for the growing army of wannabe rockers who now choose iPads over sofa pads. You're older but bolder, so don't look back over your shoulder. Grab the brass teething ring, and forge forward together, tiny hands held tightly in yours.

George Bernard Shaw said, "I want to be thoroughly used up when I die, for the harder I work, the more I live." There's wisdom in that. I've never worked harder than I have raising children, but I've never felt more fully alive. Each day is filled with new energizing action, entertaining drama, and deeper meaning.

I didn't think this depth of passion was still in me, but it sure is, and late blooming fatherhood brought it kicking out the jams and screaming back to life. My mature eyes are freshly open to look not in some smudged nostalgic rear-view mirror, but instead to envision the exhilarating road ahead, winding over hidden hills, through adventures yet to play, and toward that horizon that keeps getting pushed ever forward.

The Who said what Shaw was getting at when they screamed, "Hope I die before I get old." The Who still tours. Guess they haven't gotten old. We're talking 'bout my generation. Rock on. Raise a bit more Cain, raise the roof. Go ahead, raise some kids.

Becoming a prime time dad has turned my world up to a full blast, epic Nigel Tufnel 11.

....

SIX

YOU'RE WISER AND READY FOR THE EMOTIONAL TURBULENCE OF FATHERHOOD

Tennyson wrote: "Knowledge comes, but wisdom lingers." You've made it this far in life, into your prime time, and you've learned a few things along the way. Think back to some of the mistakes you made when you were younger. Do you think you'd make them today? Probably not.

Wisdom is the application of insight, knowledge and lessons learned through life's journey. And the more of it you have, the better it is for you and your progeny.

Being a father requires daily doses of wisdom. Every child comes with a unique set of challenges, demands and needs. Important decisions and choices must be made on a variety of fundamental issues such as safety, diet, health care, sleep, quality time, education, recreation, psychological stimulation, problem solving, to mention a few.

Smart alecks and wise guys can be brilliant, but they're not always wise. You may not know everything about parenthood, but as a mature man, you know enough to know what you do not know and how to find proper answers.

Parenthood presents diverse, tricky challenges that require careful consideration. How high should a fever be before calling the doctor? Is Cartoon Network considered bad television? How do you baby-proof the entire household? Should we get a math/reading tutor? Are electronic games really so bad? Should we bend on bedtimes, chores, and healthy eating?

There are larger issues, too, such as how to impart to your children values and qualities such as compassion, charity, good sportsmanship and citizenship, perseverance, and independent thinking. The list goes on.

Meanwhile, there's other planning and work to do in family areas such as remodeling the house for an extra bathroom or bedroom, saving for college and retirement, parental job sharing, and career and relationship changes, among many others.

I found as a late-blooming first time dad that I'd acquired a certain degree of wisdom through my years of experience, mistakes and plain old life. This wisdom is helping me meet the workload of fatherhood. I'm much better prepared now than I would have been in my 20s or 30s.

The effective application of mature wisdom will help save you from drowning in the flood of problem solving that inevitably hits new parents. As a wiser man, you're better equipped to handle whatever is thrown at you.

I look at emotional maturity as a subset of wisdom. Awareness of and control over emotions grows, gets refined, and is appropriately applied more often through the richness of experience.

Midlife men have been raked across the coals, have had their hearts broken, their anger piqued, and suppressed their tears more often than their younger brethren. They have a longer track record of emotionally-charged mistakes and missed stakes that help inform their choices of action. The word restraint is actually in a mature man's vocabulary.

Becoming a parent induces a nearly complete cognitive change that forever alters the way you will look at life. This dramatic transformation has been known to send younger, less mature men to boozy bars, fast cars and crossed stars. The prime time dad has the depth of both experience and character required to appreciate and deal with these changes in a healthy manner.

As a parent, you will never again look at the daily horror show of news in the same way. Even as a news junkie, I quickly turn the channel any time a news story hammers home an injustice done to a child. You'll empathize on a newfound gut level with the illnesses and deaths of others, the suffering caused by Mother Nature and man, the desires of parents worldwide to provide for, care for, and create better lives for their offspring.

Anyone's disoriented child shouting, "Dad!" in a crowded department store will have you turning your head to help. The cacophony of voices at a children's playground transforms into joyful music.

Ancestral roots dig deeper with meaning, the school board elections will suddenly really matter, reckless drivers will prod you to lobby City Hall for speed bumps, and the tears of other grieving parents in foreign lands will fill your own eyes.

I've been fundamentally changed at my core, improved as a human being by the heart-opening process of parenthood. And I'm grateful I was emotionally mature enough to appreciate this ongoing self-actualizing transformation.

....

SEVEN

ENJOY GREAT SEX DURING OVULATION ORGIES

This most certainly can apply to men and women of any age, but I discovered as a prime time dad that there's an ancient, almost occult skill women have for divining the best times for conception.

It has something to do with measuring menstrual cycles, lunar phases, and I'm fairly certain, reciting misty mantras about Stonehenge. But pay attention, guys, because when couples decide to get pregnant, the female of the species undergoes a monthly transformation into a determinedly sexual creature with a seemingly insatiable appetite for you.

Okay, the truth may be that she just wants your seed, but whatever your age, you might as well relax, go with the flow, and enjoy the ovulation orgy. It's prime time for jeans to drop and genes to join. Get plenty of rest, eat your oysters, saddle up, and get ready for the randy ride of life.

My advice is that you encourage your gal to really go for it. Her willingness, indeed obsession, during these critical calendar days, can be your ticket to dreams fulfilled. Invite her to dress up as a French maid or dress down like Lady Gaga. Hook up a trapeze. Break out the toys, the passion potions and the motion lotions. You get the idea. Suggest whatever lurid thoughts lurk in your libido, because she may never again be so motivated to fulfill your every fantasy.

This monthly rockin' rhythm of the ovulation orgy may be your best chance ever to live and love like Hef or Warren Beatty or plain ol' you. Just because there's a higher purpose to all the action doesn't mean you can't enjoy it.

Alright, sexual daydream time's over, boys, back to your desks. The reality of the ovulation orgy may be more like a sharp elbow poke to your ribs, her saying, "Again," and you replying, "Already?" But it's certainly real and it can certainly be real fun.

I know that all new fathers are not minted via this old-fashioned method of procreation. There are second marriages, adoptions, medical procedures, and other means. But if you're ever invited to an ovulation orgy, be careful with any video coverage. Kids are born gadget gurus. "Hey Dad, why were you dressed up as Zorro?"

EIGHT

....

BEHOLD YOUR RADIANT
PREGNANT WIFE

I t's not just young men who are superficial about women's looks. I know mature single men who will not even have coffee with a woman unless she's 20 years their junior and thin as an anorexic super model.

So, I know that many of you men reading this may think I'm either crazy or calculatingly trying to pander to my women readers, but the truth is that women are never more beautiful than when they are pregnant. Allow me to repeat that: Women are never more beautiful than when they are pregnant.

When with child, our women vibrantly glow with nature's life-enhancing hormones. They are happy, content, naturally in their element, optimistic, and sexy. Yes, sexy.

Pregnant women fill out in the most attractive voluptuous ways. Their natural feminine curves are appealingly accentuated, rounded with a ripening Rubenesque softening and shaping.

Speaking from the heart and from the locker room, you'll love the enhancing transformation nature performs on your pregnant lady. It's sure to arouse your affection... and more basic instincts.

But I think this powerful attraction action is all about the dramatic difference. In magnetism, opposites attract. If men and women are sexually attracted to one another because they are different, then pregnancy is, of course, the ultimate state of male/female contrast.

Okay guys, guffaw, shake your heads, inspect, dissect and reject my psyche, but if you want children, I hope you get the chance to savor this almost metaphysical metamorphosis in your spouse. She will dazzle you. "Vive la difference!"

NINE

....

YOU'RE NOW LESS SELF-CENTERED, MORE READY TO GIVE BACK

As younger men, we tend to take and acquire. We strive for pleasure, action, toys, power, and status. We're convinced we're right about everything, and we don't mind sharing our points of view with anyone within listening distance. That's not an evil indictment of youth. It's human, natural, the way things are in this world.

But as we mature, we find our Ptolemaic, self-centered view of existence is not only half-vast but also unsustainable. We grow increasingly aware that others exist in our world, and they matter. Immature obsession with self is unrealistic, and can become unhealthy, even toxic.

Fatherhood forces you into the larger world that exists outside the bubble of inwardly focused illusions. The prime time man is well-suited to make the necessary inclusionary adjustments that parenthood demands.

There's healthy freedom from self to be found in rocking a feverish toddler to sleep, applying *SpongeBob SquarePants* bandages to imaginary wounds, and wearing silly kid-drawn ties to work.

The man of accomplishment who trades dusty trophies for diapers evolves into a better man who wins by surrendering to become just another bench player in one of life's grandest games.

It's not for everyone. But if your personal bests and the reliving of your latest birdie just don't seem to fill that void that opens up when you close your eyes, then maybe you're ready to move forward along fatherhood's rewarding path from the poverty of me to the majesty of we.

Nothing will pull you out of self-congratulation and into the world of "give and you shall receive" like raising kids. And as a man in midlife, you probably possess enough toys, trinkets and treasures to realize that you might get the most out of the entire accumulation by selling it all on eBay.

Even those of you intently playing the game of acquisition may be finding that it's no longer as exciting as when you first started out, that the bling does not ring your chimes as it once did. Much of your stuff just gathers dust and rust.

So, if it's becoming increasingly clear that your mountain of material is merely taking up physical space and is no longer the rewarding object of your personal rat race, then it may be time to move from the acquisition stage to the sharing stage.

The guiding lights and shining stars of that sharing stage are, drum roll please, children. Don't misunderstand me. Kids will not share, unless they're trying to pawn off something nutritious. But they sure will delight in any and all you can give.

It's a Kismet cosmic connection for the prime time dad. On the one hand is a man matured beyond a focus on the material, and on the other hand are children who are endlessly needy and greedy. One hand feeds the other, and washes it, puts Band-Aids on it, removes slivers, and shoves it into baseball gloves.

The Good Books throughout the ages are right about this: we receive through giving. The more you give, the more you live. The constraints of self can actually straitjacket freedom and restrict growth. Through the selfless giving that is the inescapable daily reality of parenthood, one actually glimpses the right-sized-ego joy of freedom from self.

Giving doesn't take much effort. It's true that kids find the big cardboard box that transforms into an imaginary fort more pleasurable than the toy it contained. Your creative, attentive, mentoring, loving time is the greatest gift of all.

As a prime time man, you are now aged to perfection to give back. And you'll find that this life stage of genuine generosity actually benefits you just as much, if not more, than it does your children.

TEN

....

SAY SO LONG TO
LONELINESS

Because we've seen more highs and exhaled more sighs, the piercing pangs of loneliness sharpen with age.

As a divorced, childless man in my 40s, I had a pretty good life. I dated, had many friends from different circles, owned a home in northern California, held a leadership position in an occupation in which I excelled, saw every movie and went to any ball game I desired, vacationed, and stayed in touch with family, friends and colleagues.

Yet despite my abundance of freedom and external trappings, the truth is that there were many times when I was flat out lonely.

Sure I had the freedom to do anything anytime, but my life did not have a counterpoint that underscored and emphasized that freedom. I knew deep inside that I was missing something important in life.

There was a housing frenzy in this area when I shopped for the home in which we currently reside. I was single at the time, and really scared I might be buying into a housing bubble that could pop me back under the poverty line.

Home prices were rising every week, sometimes every day, and a swarm of eager buyers descended en masse upon every new listing that came up. Multiple bid offers pushed up the prices, cash deals were common, and it was standard operating procedure here for winning bid houses to be torn down to make room on the pricy land for new mega-sized McMansions.

I needed to figure out a way to ensure I made the right choice. So, I bought a small home that was within walking distance of two elementary schools, one middle school, a great park, and a library. My thinking was that if I could no longer afford the mortgage and upkeep, chances were that some guy with a family would want such proximity to these children's resources.

So I moved into my new home, putting my things away in every room and all the closets without a thought of leaving space for anyone else. Having lived for so long in apartments and smaller rental homes, the comparative spaciousness of this very modestly sized dwelling allowed me to leave unpacked boxes in an unused room.

I'd go to work and see parents walking their children to the nearby schools, hear the thump of the next door neighbor boy's errant baseball slamming into my wall, hand out candy to the Halloween monsters and princesses, and all of it, especially those unpacked boxes in the unused room, strummed strings of loneliness that made me long for something more, something more crowded.

It didn't take long. My humble home was first opened to my loving and lovely wife, and then over the next few years the full assault force of two healthy, hungry, hilarious children marched in to take over. I've never had a lonely moment since.

This family of mine is all here every day, jumping on the furniture, staining the carpeting, hugging me, making large and diminutive demands upon my life and schedule, and filling it with love and life and the terrific turmoil of parenthood.

I may be tired at the end of every day. I may have too many chores and not enough skill to adequately perform them. I may long for the too-short quiet stretches of time to work and write and relax, and each day is filled to the brim with blood, sweat, tears and fears. But since this infant invasion, I have not been lonely for a single moment.

Every wall in that formerly forlorn, empty room is covered with kid art from pre-school classes on up, and it now overflows with clear evidence of family life including sticky-icky easy chairs, drool-stained pillows, and cozy blankets lightly sprinkled with buttered popcorn remains.

My children and I walk hand-in-hand to that nearby school just about every day. I've endlessly pushed both kids on swings and jumped in piles of leaves in that nearby park. And I've read stories to them and watched puppet shows in the children's section of that library.

Remember my strategy about buying the house? If trouble hit, I could sell it to some guy with a family. The irony hit me like a ton of macaroni and cheese a few years later when I realized that the "some guy with a family" turned out to me!

ELEVEN

....

OLD DOGS CAN LEARN
NEW TRICKS

I want to bark and howl to the world that mid-life men are in their prime when it comes to having the right stuff to be great fathers. Why not? We certainly have the ability to become late-blooming successes in other areas of life. For instance, a not overly exhaustive Internet search reveals that:

Colonel Sanders finally franchised his Kentucky Fried Chicken at age 65. Actor Danny Aiello did not begin acting until he was 40. Ronald Reagan was first elected to public office at age 55. And Raymond Chandler published his first short story at age 45.

Okay, okay, but what does this short list of long-in-the-tooth distinguished late bloomers have to do with everyday, ordinary folks like you and me? Ask around at your next party and you'll find numerous stories of mature people making successful, major changes in their lives by joining the Peace Corps, venturing into new businesses, focusing on artistic endeavors, taking up new sports, studying a passion, and making delayed or brand new dreams come true.

Their successes underscore the point that old dogs can learn new tricks, and that mature guys can most certainly learn and love the tricks and treats of later blooming fatherhood.

Variety is the spice of life, and change is an elixir for the soul. Having children in midlife can provide the spark that ignites a new fire in the mature man's heart, enlightening and invigorating him to a rewarding and rejuvenating new stage of creative existence.

New things can be thrilling and they can be chilling. Fatherhood induces both. In the early years of my dad journey, this ol' dog was tentative. I was so uncertain, even fearful about my ability to deal with the barrage of unique situations coming at me that I psychologically retreated into my imaginary doghouse. I'd poke my nose out to sniff the surroundings, leave the canine confines to do what was necessary, and then quickly retreat back inside.

But fatherhood's new leash on my life actually gave me a new lease on life. Like the learning curve for any new activity, the more I successfully dealt with challenging situations, the more I explored outside of my doghouse, and the more abundant and fulfilling life became.

If you're a middle-aged man, chances are you've focused your professional life on one or two basic lines of specialized work and maybe three to six different jobs. Almost immediately upon parenthood, you'll try your hand at multiple new jobs. You'll be able to dabble at or become adept at such diverse occupations as safety inspector, short order cook, fashion consultant, teacher, coach, healthcare provider, chauffeur, product analyzer, mediator, nutritionist, art critic, psychologist, and pack horse, among others. Talk about resume padding.

The list of new things I've seen, done, and learned as a prime time dad is endless, and the process of learning and living the myriad endeavors required of parenthood keeps me on my toes and reaching high. Whether I'm sent to the Internet to research how to build a Pinewood Derby car or learn CPR or study investment strategies for college costs, the tasks keep me growing, informed, and alert.

The greatest thing about these jobs is that you'll be motivated not by money but by the heart. These are indeed labors of love, and you won't be watching the clock or counting the days until vacation. You'll explore and learn and succeed as a natural course of caring for your children. In the manner of that Peace Corps commercial, these are the toughest jobs you'll ever love.

The ultimate surprise parenthood revealed to me was that of experiencing love on a much deeper level. I was not ignorant of love and feelings. I understood, even studied, some basic poetics of the human heart, and always thought of myself as being perceptive when it came to empathizing with others. But I never really understood the profound level of love that parents feel for their children until I became a dad.

Parental love changes the world into a new frontier where ordinary life transforms into opportunities for unforeseen danger or unique surprise. Everyday life demands new attention, from the speeding car to the aspirin in the non-safety capped bottle to the staircase to the steak knife inadvertently left on a table.

And joyful discoveries abound, from your child's smiles of recognition to the smiles of strangers when your child tantrums to the wonder of a ladybug to the sliding magic of an ordinary carpet rug.

Parenthood is life renewed. It is about keeping your head above water in an endless stream of newness. When I can dog paddle along with the flow of the stream's current, it focuses, energizes, challenges, stimulates and refreshes me.

Instead of us older dogs rolling over, scratching our genitalia and napping, we can sink our teeth deeply into the marrow of the family pork chop bone, snatch it up and run fast with it, not over the hill, but up into the sunlight. Bark on, prime time dad, do not play dead.

Section II.

Off and Running

TWELVE

....

NEVER AGAIN BE BORED

As the years add up, the body may languish and the spirit can fade. That spontaneous joy of life often diminishes under the weary weight of repetition, routine, and responsibility.

Maybe we haven't achieved all the goals we set out to accomplish. The defeats, disappointments, and death of our dreams can form a grey cloud of resigned desperation that follows us, rumbling now and then, threatening rain, reminding us of our clay feet and the finite number of steps we have.

Boredom is a tricky subject. I don't claim to know your inner world, and I won't trespass there. But, I will share a bit about mine. During my childless years, I never wanted to admit to being plagued by boredom's advancing grey monotony.

I ran around like crazy, scheduling events with friends, traveling, dating, dining, and staying busy in a Mobius strip race to keep in check the hollow humdrum gnawing I felt growing inside.

With too much time on my hands and ennui edging out spontaneous joy, I found myself on dates or in leisurely coffee cafes admiring not my companions or my good fortune, but the couples I saw haplessly tangled up in toddler gear.

Sure, these new parents fumbled, fumed and fought with their new predicaments and them-selves, but it seemed to me they were engaged in something special, something all consuming and truly meaningful.

Then lightening struck, and I was to become a father. My world was forever charged with a pow-erful new electrifying current that positively re-pelled the negative state of boredom.

To give you one of thousands of examples of eye-opening newness, let's take a random walk down Daddy Drive and think about... okay, I've got it. Let's start very near the beginning, with the birthing process itself.

Do childless men know anything about what re-ally goes on at childbirth? While it's standard operating procedure to the health practitioners who bring newborns into the world, it sure was an eye-opener to me.

My wife Lucy was in labor with our first child in April of 2000. Since this was not the era of the husband-is-out-in-the-lobby-smoking-a-cigar, I was dutifully all present and accounted for in the labor room dreading what was coming down the chute, so to speak.

Nervously awaiting the right dilation lotto numbers to hit, I looked up from the magazine I hid behind to view a most unexpected, vividly searing, definitely not boring sight. Our labor nurse was busy applying gobs of lubricating ointment to my wife's most private, personal parts.

She told us it would help promote stretching to prevent tearing during the rigors of childbirth. The nurse was absolutely matter of fact about the process, and since my wife had an epidural to diminish the feeling below her waist, she could not feel the attentions that had me so mesmerized from my front row seat.

This nurse was ever so thoroughly conscientious. She slowly, methodically, tenderly massaged the slippery jell onto, into, and around and around and around.

I watched transfixed. I'd been to a few men's joints in my days, but I'd never seen this one before. Was it some violation of our wedding vows? I mean, wasn't I the one who should be performing this particular K-Y duty? Maybe I should stand up and tell the nurse, "Good start, but I'll take it from here. Let me show you how it's done, I know what she really likes."

The procedure was clinical, of course, but cursed or blessed with an active libidinous imagination, I found it hypnotizingly erotic. So, there in the cold sterility of a birthing station filled with medical equipment, awaiting the arrival of my first child, a spiritual milestone one should use to ponder the mysterious majesty of life, love and the universe, I felt arousal's insistent rising tide.

How twisted can you get? I thought, quickly damning myself. Immediately ashamed and to get my mind on other, more pedestrian matters, I tried to lobby the nurse about what I'd be doing when the time came.

"I guess I'll be up here, by her head, helping with her breathing, right?" I ventured, hoping for an easy assignment.

She replied matter-of-factly, "There are only two of us and she has two legs. You'll grab one leg and push." That did the trick. I was back in the real world, but this real world was no longer the same. And it was not boring.

I stood awestruck at the gateway of this intriguing new world filled with unanticipated events, emotions and possibilities that unfolded naturally before my eyes. The realization of the unfathomable uniqueness that lay ahead of me, along with the star of the opening act, was slowly emerging.

I'm telling you from personal experience that the dark existential boredom cloud that can hover over midlife men can be transitory. Prime time fatherhood was the lightning strike that stripped off my dark shades, illuminated a new way for me to see the world, and ignited a passionate, roaring blaze in my heart.

THIRTEEN

....

TRANSFORM FLEDGING WRINKLES INTO LAUGH LINES

Somber studies show that those who laugh more, live longer. It seems laughter is indeed a potent medicine that helps keep us healthy, thriving, and sane. As a prime time dad, you'll need plenty of this mirthful elixir to keep you right-side up. And the good news is that your medicine cabinet will be well stocked.

Parenthood gives us ample opportunity to laugh. As a midlife man, you've seen and experienced much, and as a result, you have a solid sense of the many meandering mazes that make up life's path. This mature perspective will help you perceive the humor in otherwise troubling situations.

It's funny – not ha ha funny, but interesting funny – that we parents easily laugh when we see a tantrumming toddler tormenting a parent, but seldom see the humor when it happens to us. It's a perverse human trait that allows us to laugh at the man slipping on a banana peel. We're glad it's not us. Tragedy happens to me, while comedy happens to you.

The week before our son was born, I was a carefree expectant dad driving leisurely around town with my wife looking for a restaurant we'd heard was simply fabulous. Two days after our son was born, I was again driving around, this time through strange neighborhoods, in a rush and near panic trying to find the home of a woman who rented industrial-strength breast pumps.

Yes, that's right, industrial-strength breast pumps. My darling wife would not countenance regular breast pumps, which I knew absolutely nothing about, but that, as I understand it, are sold under-the-counter and out of normal human view in most drug stores. No, my bride, the mother of my first bouncing baby needed the industrial-strength model, which she had been told, didn't break down.

Now, for you uninitiated out there, breast pumps are not some device *Maxim* models use to pump up their cleavage or get their nipples erect before an oiled-up photo shoot. Simply put, a breast pump is a cow-milking machine for human women. They vacuum out a steady supply of breast milk for later bottle-feeding use.

My son's breastfeeding latch was not yet perfected, and we needed the machine to ensure a plentiful supply of breast milk. It was a weekend, but there was no way this newly minted dad would not succeed in getting food into his newborn son's mouth. This was an important mission, not like merely remembering to pick up a loaf of bread or get the car's oil changed. This had elements of real life drama, eat or starve, live or die stuff. Can do, I thought.

The industrial-strength breast pump lady operated out of her home, and I sat on a wet, sticky couch in her chaotic living room that had been completely overtaken by four or five screaming toddlers who jumped all over the furniture and ran about like hyper-excited monkeys in the movies.

What was she doing with so many kids the same age? I thought. Obviously, they were not all siblings. The environment sure didn't seem like a day care situation. Maybe, because she was the industrial-strength breast pump lady, she spent her days pumping prodigious amounts of breast milk and served it to the entire neighborhood. I'm glad she did not offer me something to drink.

I was given a quick, noisy, constantly interrupted course in the pump's operations, what tubes attach where, how it should be worn, what to expect. I couldn't fathom a word. It was worse than looking underneath the hood of today's computerized cars. And *The Ransom of Red Chief* kids scared me. I wanted out of there as fast as possible, so I wrote the check and ran. Mission accomplished.

Back at home, I tried to play the returning hero bringing in the hard won prize, but my mother-in-law was staying with us for a couple weeks, and since her daughter had just gone through the real ordeal of delivering a child, I quickly realized that I didn't have an audience willing to consider, let alone applaud, my Herculean efforts.

Somehow the women knew which suction cup went where and how the tubes attached to the device and the bottles, and the pump seemed to work, so they brusquely ushered me out of the inner sanctum. I was happy to leave them, knowing my son would now get his fair share of the super nutritious colostrum and breast milk.

However, this peace of mind was shattered an hour or so later when I walked past the child's room and saw the reality horror-show of my exhausted passed-out wife snoring loudly while attached to this milking machine as it huffed and sucked meager spurts of life's elixir into two little plastic bottles.

I knew intellectually that women's breasts were designed for this natural purpose, of course, but watching this scene deeply disturbed me, like when I first learned on the playground how babies were really made. "My parents would never do that," I remember saying.

In my mind, the sight of this noisy, foreign apparatus mechanically sucking on my wife's breasts was so unexpected, so incongruous, that she might've been abducted by aliens on a mission to extract specimens from female earthlings before worm-holing back to their star system.

I stared as I might at a horrible car accident, then quickly looked away. But it was hopeless. The image stayed with me. Senses shocked, basic sexual instincts rocked, I longed for the therapeutic trance of an old Russ Meyer film to get my equilibrium back.

You gotta laugh or you'll go nuts when your son pees a perfect arc into your ear during diapering. I argue that one must develop a keen sense of humor to survive parenthood, and I truly believe that because I was a midlife father, I had a longer and richer perspective from which to draw upon the raw material required to perform the mental tricks that turn tragedy into comedy.

FOURTEEN

····································

YOU CAN SPEND MORE TIME WITH THE KIDS IN THEIR FORMATIVE YEARS

The most formative years for children are in their first four to six years of life. This is the time when they gain confidence for living and learning primarily through a close relationship with their parents. Both parents.

Since you're in your prime years and a bit more mature, it's more likely that you have achieved some degree of success, skill, and trusted longevity in your workday life. With that success comes more freedom of choice, more freedom of time, more loosening of the job tether.

As compared with a man just beginning to make his mark, you are more apt to be able to spend a bit more quality time with your youngsters. You probably have the freedom to spend one morning per week at pre-school. You may be able to initiate flex time or work remotely to decrease your hours toiling at the office in order to spend more quality time at home helping with the child rearing or coaching or club activities. You might be able to become a consultant with more flexible hours, or work part time for a stretch, or take a sabbatical, or decide to write that book that's kept you tossing and pacing at night.

I spent the first year of my son's life pounding out mileage on the Silicon Valley treadmill, and many of those "missing dad" clichés came true for me. I missed his first eating of solid food, the first time he crawled, when he learned to bounce in the doorjamb jumping contraption, and of course, I missed his first steps.

We sold the agency where I worked, and like all good wage slaves, I immediately began to scour the marketplace for another position. But my heart was not in it. Knowing that I might not be around late into my son's life, I increasingly wanted to be resolutely and undeniably there for him (and later, for my daughter) during his early formative years.

So, with a wee cash cushion from my years of toiling on Maggie's Farm, I decided to earn money by consulting, work on my long-denied dream of writing books and screenplays, and spend much more time with my kids at home.

Frankly, I wasn't quite prepared for the shock of the transition. It was truly strange to be out in the world during the daytime without having a business purpose. I felt out of place, a bit freakish, certainly self-conscious. I suspected the mothers watching me push my son on the park swing thought I was a loser, a pervert, Aqua Lung, or worse, a grandfather!

I consoled myself with the knowledge that I was doing this for my kids. Come embarrassment, self-pity, or ineptitude, they darn well were going to know their dad and that their dad was a familiar, accessible, looming and loving presence in their lives.

With the usual bumps and detours found in any new journey, it's all working out. The moms in the park warmed up to me after awhile, especially as they discovered we all share the same levels of parental exasperation, frustration, and exhilaration.

I've been more productive as a writer and business consultant than I ever anticipated.

I've moved through the self-conscious stage of hands-on fatherhood, and found that the vast majority of friends and colleagues out there respect my choices. There are an increasing number of fathers, young and mature, doing or contemplating doing the exact same thing.

Whatever manifestation of freedom your years on the job have afforded you, as a mature man, it's likely you'll have more flexibility than younger parents to wrangle precious time to spend with your children when they are young, the most critical period of their development.

Early time with both parents helps children feel truly appreciated, attached, and centered, and builds their self esteem. This freedom of choice and time can make all the difference in the world to your children and to you.

FIFTEEN

....

FIGHT ALZHEIMER'S DISEASE?

What? Having children can strike a blow against Alzheimer's Disease? Increasing evidence suggests that keeping your brain active by learning challenging new things may help stave off the advance of this debilitating disease. Studies show that one activity well suited to this is the learning of a new language. So, with my foreign-language-elocution tongue poised firmly in cheek, here's my bit.

You will be bombarded by a bewildering crush of new language as a prime time father. First lesson: go to a pre-natal course with your partner. Your head will reel at the discussions of placental afterbirth, umbilical cord registry, in utero meconium aspiration, and birth canal elasticity. I came out of these classes ripped and raring to go—into therapy!

Then, the home front must be prepared. Learn about diapers and lotions, organic food, mixing formula, freezing breast milk, and wearing Baby Bjorns in the front, back packs in the rear.

Follow Esperanto-like instructions for the "simple" assembly of baby strollers and cribs, and the installation of baby-proofed gates and latches and locks and car safety seats.

And as your wife or partner searches online for Megan's Law creeps, you can view DVDs of your new life's horror movies: what to do if your child is choking, swallows poison, or needs CPR. Is your mind waving at its cobwebs, yet?

Since you'll want to model proper language usage to your newborn, you must carefully review each sentence and utterance before speaking, lest the salty lingo and slangy sloppiness from the hockey games and poker nights of your childless days scorch tender ears. This mental pre-emptive editing will keep your overwhelmed brain busy.

You're finally ready to read *Goodnight Moon* to that infant who sleeps all day and cries all night, putting your mind on alert 'til dawn. And don't forget the mental strain applied to deciphering your child's first attempts at language. "I want shhuuzzerrpoddsssty," can have you running around for everything from a squeeze toy to the portable potty to strained sausage sushi.

And you can look forward to future homework-helping years of mental gymnastics prodded by yet the latest version of "new math," the unveiling of recent scientific discoveries and technological innovations, and the secret intricacies needed to crack the technological codes of evolving social networking.

Having children will keep your mind active in a non-stop effort to learn the new languages of parenthood. There are no CliffsNotes short cuts, the work cannot be performed by a tutor, and you'll be tested every day. But this new language is the exquisite music of life itself, although I can't quite remember why I wanted to avoid forgetting.

- - - - - - - - - - - - - - -

If you're not in immediate need of relief due to my fracturing of the funny bone, it's now time for something completely similar.

Yes, it's true that most children's book typefaces are rather large, so as a prime time dad, you won't need your reading glasses to help your young ones drift off to your melodious interpretations of their nighttime favorites.

But it is not true, wise guy, that diapers can be substituted for Depends, and that baby food is a healthy soft chew choice for false-teeth-wearing geezers.

No, midlife dads do not take simultaneous naps with their kids (although it would be heavenly), and our night-night bedtimes are not synchronized.

Tiny tot night lights do not turn on by clapping, and toddler strollers are too small to help the mobility of infirm adults.

For the record, we prime time dads do not drool more copiously than our kids, and while our heads are covered by about the same amount of sparse hair, we can grow it much more effectively from our ears!

SIXTEEN

....

THERE'S LOTS MORE
HELP OUT THERE NOW

For those of you who tend toward the tough, taciturn, take-care-of-things-yourself type, you may find it peculiar, even weak, to survey the wide range of ubiquitous help being offered to new parents. Then again, you may be surprised at how foreign a realm is fatherhood.

For example, let's go back to the subject of breastfeeding. Our son was placed on Lucy's breast for feeding right after being born. Sounds like one of the most natural things in the world, right? Actually, successful breastfeeding can be a tricky and delicate dance for both mother and child.

Lucy didn't know what she was doing, and unlike his dad, my baby son hadn't encountered this situation before. The nurse tried to help with quick advice, but she was busy, and it's really a dynamic the duo must resolve together. Bottom line, he got a bad latch and Lucy got an inflamed nipple.

Okay, okay, if you've never had kids, this all sounds like a stubbed toe. But an inflamed nipple can hurt, it can become infected which means the baby may get less of the super nutritious breast milk, and it may also mean that mom and baby are not mastering the feeding fundamentals, which can lead to more serious health problems.

Brave Lucy sucked it up and sucked it out with the industrial-strength breast pump for several days, but her inflamed nipple got worse, and one of her breasts simply refused to go with the flow.

So we went to a lactation consultant. I was hoping to peruse a thick book of vivid before and after photos of several subjects to help me better understand the process, but what we got, after waiting several days to get an appointment at the thriving consultancy, was clearer directions on how to fix and empty Lucy's engorged breast and fill up our boy's growling tummy.

Armed with new knowledge and a special lubricating lotion that farmers rub on cows' udders, yes, utterly true, we went confidently forth as a family that wouldn't need Enfamil.

When my parents raised me, they read advice from the book *Dr. Spock's Baby and Child Care*, and relied upon the limited guidance of hand-me-down bromides such as "Spare the rod and spoil the child." (Old news flash: Spanking is no longer a recommended disciplinary activity.)

By comparison, today's prime time fathers have an abundance of resources to help them steer through the tricky shoals of the child rearing process. As the linkages solidify between early childhood care and the future health/happiness of the child, there's grown a thriving industry of social and business enterprises devoted to kid care.

It's not just the libraries, book sellers, and websites stocked with literature on every conceivable aspect of nurturing children. Help also takes the form of: adult educational classes and lectures; an explosion of daycare, nanny care and live-in care options; exercise, sports and activity options for the kids that begin before their first birthday; a plethora of pre-school and educational opportunities; religious reading and social programs; diaper and food services that deliver to the door; health care advocacy training programs; party consultants and entertainers; personal trainers, personal shoppers, and if you look hard and long enough even, maybe, an old-fashioned neighborhood babysitter. The list goes on an on.

Parents today are not in this alone, although post-partum blues and newborn monitoring isolation can sometimes make it seem that way. Today's dad can call in the cavalry with a quick Internet search or by looking up the child help services in the phone book, community directory, websites of local schools and hospitals, YMCA or religious order of choice.

You'll find a community of like-minded parents associated with each organization filled with professionals who can help with just about any aspect of parenting. Tap into these varied networks, and enjoy the social, psychological, and educational benefits they offer.

As children's play dates become group therapy sessions for parents, you'll find that the kindred-spirited camaraderie of parents will lighten your load, and make it easier to learn how to make the right child-rearing decisions that you probably won't be able to follow anyway.

SEVENTEEN

....

SEX IN YOUR FIRST
YEAR OF FATHERHOOD

....

EIGHTEEN

HANG OUT WITH A YOUNGER CROWD

As a later in life dad, I definitely worried about how younger, more traditionally-aged new parents would view me. Would they think I was the grandfather? Would they slip me some extra diapers thinking I might need Depends for uncontrolled urine drip? Would they look at my yawn and quickly throw me a boppy pillow expecting me to drop my head into a fast drooling sleep like Homer Simpson's dad?

As I've repeated so many times you may think I suffer from short term memory loss, none of those fears ever materialized. Yes, most (but not all) of my fellow new parents were at least a decade or more younger than me, but parenthood levels all fields.

The common bonds and mutual desires to succeed as parents bind us in a kid kinship that sees beyond age, station, and creed. I have always been accepted by these younger parents, always, and contrary to my paranoia, many of them have expressed to me their sincere admiration for my journey.

Several years back, I experienced the psychological breakthrough that provided healing insight into my age issues. We invited two other couples and their children over for a cookout. During the course of the evening, all the kids followed my then three-year-old son's lead of stripping off his clothes and running wild and naked around the house and yard.

The kids were squealing with joy and having a riot. I was a bit concerned that some of our parent guests might object to this permissive nudist romp, so I asked gently if everything was okay.

One of the young moms, barely 30 years old at the time, smiled knowingly to me and warmly said, "We just love coming to your house. It's like Woodstock!"

Wow. Her words warmed me like hot chocolate on the ski slope. This wonderful woman was not even alive when Woodstock surprised the world with "the New York State Thruway is closed, man," yet her reference reminded and reassured me that we parents share a common lot regardless of our external differences, and that parenthood, at any point of life, bonds us.

In just a few brief moments of reflection on her kind, inclusive words, I happily experienced the healing transformation of feeling fully and completely accepted.

I realized that not one of my younger parent friends had ever discriminated against me because of my age. They'd always treated me as an equal, just another new dad, bumbling and researching, trying to figure out how to do what's best for the children.

All my fears were unfounded. It was all inside my own crazy head. I'd tortured myself by comparing my insides to their externals. I had been the ageist! This was a revelation for me. I now openly and honestly discuss my age when occasions arise. A 33-year-old father of two recently confided to me that he secretly felt too young for fatherhood.

I genuinely like this younger crowd. They're dedicated, non-judgmental, entrepreneurial, and open to new ideas about parenting and life. I'm energized in their presence, and grateful to have finally realized I was diminishing my own enjoyment of fatherhood by worrying about age.

As medical science advances and social stigmas decline, the number of prime time dads grows. There are more and more of us every year. I've found complete support and acceptance from the younger parents in our play date, pre- and elementary school, sports activities and social circles.

I've come to understand that my fears about being outside the norm were a result of my own lack of acceptance of myself as a later blooming dad. It's an inside job. No one else seems to care. These younger parents helped teach me to feel more comfortable in my own, slightly more weathered, skin.

I decided to seize the daze and embrace becoming a doting, not doddering, prime time dad.

NINETEEN

....

FINALLY GET YOUR HOME THEATER CRANKING

Having children may be the best excuse I know for finally getting your home entertainment theater up and cranking. Since you're spending lots more time at your crib tending to the kids, varnishing chests of drawers, baby proofing the house, rocking a sick and sleepless child, and crashing on the sofa, you might as well make the best of it.

While rewarding beyond anything I've ever done, parenthood is not a non-stop E ticket excursion. The truth is, my wife and I rarely have the time, coordinated schedules, babysitting support, and energy to get out to do the many fun things we used to enjoy in the ancient era known as BC (before children).

That especially applies to one of our favorite shared activities, going to the movies. We used to go to just about all the films worth seeing, but that action stopped the moment our first child became the feature presentation. And since I write screenplays, this lack of movie time truly limited emersion into my own art.

Despite my desire to see and study film, and despite the fact that I actually have a small office at home with room for a decent television, I did not pull the trigger on new video technology until many years into fatherhood when my old tube set finally blinked and rolled and died.

Waiting was such a mistake. The new flat panel, high definition sets transform the home movie viewing experience. The color, detail, and sound are rich, the cable selection choices many and varied, and I can stop everything, nuke some popcorn, and restart the dream right where I left it. I've not even mentioned the newfound clarity of watching sports. I can now see the puck!

Don't make the same mistake I made. Get your home theater cranking as soon as possible. Think of the thrill of finally going into the flat screen section of your electronic retailer not as a "Looky Lou" but as a real buyer on the hunt for the perfect beast to drag back to your man cave.

Go ahead, splurge. Convince your spouse. She'll need the diversion just as much, if not more, than you. Go get your own super-sized screen, mega-phonic, multidimensional, turbo-techno, Jujube entertainment enclave, and be ready to cocoon and crash and collapse in front of it when you two are three.

- - - - - - - - - - - - - - -

So, my office/man cave was taking shape. I'd set up my desk and computer station for work, and placed my go-to books nearby in my own book-shelf. My favorite photos, art, and Cleveland Browns banners were strategically hung on the walls. And the high-def TV remote was easily reachable from any reclined position of my most comfy chair. What could possibly go wrong in the sanctity of this daddy den?

The invasion started so innocently that it was unnoticeable. A simple pre-school painting here, a hand-print plaster mold there, a homemade Fa-ther's Day card taped to the desk, and a stuffed an-imal left on the end table. Floods begin with scattered raindrops.

93

Enjoying the elation on their faces as I admired their work, I eagerly (and witlessly) joined in, attaching their artwork to every available space on the walls, windows, and chimney bricks. There must be 35 pieces of children's objets d'art on my glass windows alone. No pure sunlight comes in. It's filtered through impressionistic apple trees, a drawing of Santa Claus, and a note reading, "I'm sorry Dad."

I'm pretty sure my willing participation in this stealth attack on my man cave was due to some parental variation of the Stockholm syndrome, in which hostages develop sympathy and positive feelings toward their captors.

Sure it was pleasant for a while. But the demands kept increasing. I was feeding an endlessly hungry beast. There was soon no room for my personal things.

I wrote a film script based on an old photograph of me posed with a bunch of friends at Mt. Rushmore in our longhaired days. I couldn't find a space on the wall to hang it, even if I could find the treasured shot. The kids borrowed scissors and tape and pens and rulers. I've never seen these items again.

My books are now buried in the deepest caverns of the shelves, pushed into obscurity by children's stories and family photo albums and toys and (I just now looked to see) an old electronic baby crib monitor we haven't used for nine years.

The kids have taken over. They're on my recliner, watching sports and Disney, leaving a trail of popcorn kernels, dirty socks, and half-filled water glasses.

My last and final refuge, not just in my man cave but in the entire house, is the chair in front of my computer, the one in which I now sit. But they love spinning around in it. "What's this big screw that fell off, dad?" And they can now email me, text me.

They're coming. I see the future. They're dropping sugary drinks onto my keyboard. They're holding hands with boyfriends and girlfriends, blithely waving off my warnings of safety. They're coming with outstretched hands asking for car keys, credit cards, college tuition, mortgage down payments. They're relentless. Oh yes, I know they're coming.

TWENTY

··

YOU'RE OLD ENOUGH
TO ACT LIKE A CHILD

B eing locked into the restrictive strait jacket of image is for younger folks who have the energy to worry about their hair styles, what nightclub is hot, and the latest new greatest.

For the most part, midlife men have moved through this superficial terrain, and possess the perspective to look at their formerly held-fast fads and fashionable beliefs with a backward-glancing sense of humor.

I maintain that we prime time men can laugh at ourselves a bit more easily (maybe because there's a longer record of bewildering personal behavior to inspire us), and in general, we are less fearful of the perceived social consequences of acting silly.

Are we fools, then? Au contraire, we've learned, been burned, and we're wiser. And this willingness to shed decorum is manna from heaven for our children.

Want to make your young kids laugh? Act like you almost slipped on a banana peel. That's right. We're not talking about sophisticated humor. We're talking about funny faces, prat falls, and playing down to the audience. Kids love it. And I contend that prime time men are well equipped to play the clown and allow their imaginations to soar.

Early on in fatherhood, I was at a local park with my son. The dominant play structure was a large conglomeration of jungle gym type apparatus in the vague shape of a sailing ship.

Many kids were playing on this ship shape, screaming, and having a riot. But I noticed curiously, just about all of them were playing individually. I looked around to see their parents standing nearby, texting, talking on cell phones, chatting with one another.

I wanted to engage my son in play so I decided to become Captain Hook on a pirate ship. I climbed to the top of the ship and bellowed, "I'm Captain Hook, and I'm looking for the Lost Boys."

My son immediately joined the game and ran laughing away from the horrible Captain Hook as I chased him throughout the play structure. Other lost boys and girls quickly joined in. They banded together to turn the tables and chase me. I'd run away to escape, climbing throughout the ship, then suddenly turn around to face and chase them again as they ran off squealing with surprise and laughter. In a few minutes, just about every one of the 30 or so kids was playing the game with us. It was a blast.

I took a moment to catch my breath, and looked out to see a crowd of adults watching me. I worried momentarily that they might think I was the local playground pervert or a modern day Pied Piper luring their kids off to some new Chucky Cheese franchise. But instead they smiled at me with thanks and, I sensed, a touch of silent admiration. Even better, my son seemed proud of me.

My children's hearty, high-pitched laughter is truly the sweetest sound I've ever heard. It lightens all loads, and keeps me acting silly in an ongoing effort to elicit more.

This mature man's ability to damn convention and capture your children's imagination with child-like humor and play provides pure joy to their lives. It's the super glue that bonds your relationships with your kids, and it might just add the magic of pixie dust to your life. You may not be able to fly, but you can soar.

TWENTY-ONE

....

FULFILL YOUR NEED
FOR MORE MEANING IN
LIFE

Plato is credited with saying, "The spiritual eyesight improves as the physical eyesight declines." As we mature, many of us increasingly require more meaning in life. We seek it in healthy ways such as spiritual growth and charitable endeavors, and we seek it in unhealthy ways such as flings, substance abuse, and out-of-control consumerism.

Becoming a parent is arguably one of the most meaningful roles of this mortal coil. A fresh, frail human life is inextricably in your care. It's serious business. Nurturing, teaching, and guiding a child through the passage of time is worth the struggle. Little triumphs and minor tragedies will hit you with a power you could not have imagined. Why? Because these life moments truly mean something.

Most midlife individuals have some experience with the deaths of relatives, parents, and friends. You know you are mortal and that life as we know it does not go on without end. Many of you have lived long enough to know that life in the office cubicle may not provide you the depth of meaning for which you increasingly yearn.

My younger brother, Paul, died unexpectedly when my son was 18 months old. I got the news over the telephone, made a call to verify, and when the tragedy fully sank in, cried to the universe.

Our son, who'd been napping, walked into the room where I roamed and moaned, and stared at me in surprise. He'd never before seen his huge hulking dad so distraught, wailing, and broken-hearted. He sensed something was horribly wrong. I saw his confused eyes searching mine as fear flowed over him.

Without trying to compose myself, I blurted through tears, "Uncle Paul is dead." It was my way of letting him know what was going on so he would not worry, and to bide myself some time to gather my thoughts and postpone daddy chores for a bit.

Then my son did something I'll never forget. No longer afraid, he ran to me, and hugged my legs as tight as he could. Only a year and one-half old, he was comforting and supporting his dad in this time of need.

I was amazed. Astonished by this intuitional act of compassion and grateful for his kindness, I held him close, loving him deeply. My heart melted into his arms.

I knew in those few soulful moments that everything really was going to be alright. Sure, a major milestone had been reached. The actively written book on my brother Paul was finished. But I had this new family, a new beginning, a new history to live.

Life was re-circulating. I've never before or since been as movingly consoled and restored to spiritual wholeness as that day when my toddler son instinctively hugged me back to healthy optimism.

His surprising show of human empathy drove home to me that I was truly on an amazing journey, one on which I could learn at least as much as

I taught, and that if I were wise, I'd better observe closely and engage fully.

Over the following months, our boy witnessed the close cluster of additional deaths of my father-in-law and my mother. He was still young, not yet three, and didn't inquire much about what was going on with these major life changes in our family.

Then one day, prompted by watching the demise of the character Mufasa in *The Lion King* animated movie, he asked me about death.

Hoping to avoid a heavy conversation that I was simply not prepared for and that I feared might inadvertently inflict lasting emotional scars, I told him, "Oh, cartoon characters never really die." He seemed satisfied with that answer, matter-of-factly went back to whatever he was doing, and I was happy to have avoided another potential parental minefield.

A year or so after that, our usually active son was sitting on the couch unusually quiet, even pensive. He seemed to be contemplating something serious. I asked him what was up.

"Dad," he answered, "I wish I was a cartoon character." Having forgotten our earlier conversation, I asked him, "Why?"

"Because," he said, "cartoon characters never die."

It hit me like a ton of bricks. These children see and listen and pick up what's happening in their lives. They heroically struggle to understand and make sense of their world and the places in it they occupy. And despite their brave, defiant acts of evolving independence, they have deep fears, doubts, and uncertainties, just like the rest of us.

This was a fatherly moment with him, and I took some time to paint in broad strokes my thoughts, feelings, and beliefs about death and dying. I don't think he really understood what I was saying, I don't claim to understand it myself, but he knew without a doubt that I had taken the time to discuss this subject and his concerns personally, respectfully, and lovingly. That's what was needed.

The prime time dad naturally brings to fatherhood a more reflective philosophical point of view that is conducive to raising happy, thriving children, and to putting more thoughtful smiles on parents in the process.

I truly believe that this mature stage of a man's life, when he looks more deeply into the majesty, mystery, and intrinsic value of life, is an excellent time to raise children. It's taken me on a journey to the center of meaning in my life.

Because we've lived through more of life's tragedies, I think the prime time dad can sense more deeply the special nature of life's spirit as it courses through our children's lives. We more fully recognize life's precious value because we've experienced more of its fragility, variety, and terminality.

Section III.

Establishing a Rhythm

TWENTY-TWO

....

YOU HAVE MORE
PATIENCE AND
EMPATHY

Patience is a virtue learned over time, and frankly, raising children takes more patience than any human being actually possesses. Meeting the demands of parenthood requires an almost Zen-like approach to patience. While this is impossible to achieve all the time, most of us who've sprouted a few grey hairs are certainly more patient than we were in our younger days. And that trait will make you a more effective father and a happier dad.

The secret to patience is empathy. When you realize that your child is just two feet tall, completely dependent upon you for life itself, can't perform any of the activities he or she watches you do with ease, and has a growing need to become an individual entity with intrinsic power, then you may be a bit more apt to smile and patiently help with the fourth change of clothes or read the same silly book for the tenth time or reply "After awhile crocodile," to the newly discovered alligator prompt.

Okay, it's mea culpa, full disclosure time. This is how empathy for my children was really driven home to me. The night our daughter was born, her then three-year-old brother and I went out to eat with another dad and his son. The kids were wild in the restaurant, running around noisily, not eating the expensive food we had ordered, and generally ruining our dinner and my celebratory mood.

Making matters worse, despite our grown-up protestations, both boys kept grabbing and chewing handfuls of choking-hazard candies from the tray by the cash register. (Still can't believe a kid-friendly restaurant would leave those candies within reach. Vigilance, dads, always.)

I was preoccupied with how my wife and newborn were doing, and I pleaded with my son to stop all the madness, hoping he might understand the significance of the evening. Of course, he was three, and I might just as well have expected him to understand Latin verb conjugations.

It'd been a long, stressful day, and I was tired and irritable. I grabbed him by the arm and yanked him out of the restaurant. He cried in the car all the way home. I became more frustrated, more filled with righteous anger. Didn't he know how special this day was? I dragged him to his room, practically threw him on his bed, and yelled at him to obey and behave.

The youngster was terrified. He was frozen with fear, uncertain what to do next. Then he vomited all over himself.

I stopped, looked at the situation, controlled myself, and saw him for what he was, just a three-year-old boy having fun, and then this angry giant began pulling on him and yelling at him in ways he'd never before experienced.

With his mom in the hospital with a new baby, he may have even thought he was being replaced or demoted by his new sister. He was frightened, bewildered, momentarily lost, and he didn't know what to do or where to turn. His body puked out its inability to process all these emotions.

My heart melted. I was deeply ashamed. I hugged him close, kissed him, cleaned him up, and vowed to my highest self that I'd never again even remotely manhandle my kids in any way. And I've been able to live up to that promise. I learned empathy.

Kids need patient parents, and it's not easy and oftentimes impossible to oblige. But I'm much more patient as a prime time dad than I would have been as a parent in my 20s and 30s. In those years, I would have been a terribly distracted, anxious, uninvolved parent.

Youth disdains patience, and thank goodness you're now old enough to know better.

TWENTY-THREE

....

CHANGE PAST TIMES TO
FIRST TIMES

Remember the first time you went to a drive-in movie, kissed a girl, had a birthday party, lost a tooth, ate liver, or purchased a car? We all have a long list of firsts.

But as we mature, truly unique first-ever events come around less frequently, they become scarce. We develop a tendency to reminisce about past firsts rather than create new ones. Some of the fun in life fades when there are few new firsts to live.

And if you're remotely like me, late at night in restless sleep, the thoughts rise into consciousness that, come hellfire and damnation, the game is not yet over and there still must be fun and adventure to be had. My answer arrived when I became a midlife dad.

Children row, row, row their boats down a stream of firsts. When you have kids, this unique parade of life's firsts marches briskly forward with almost daily revelations.

First smiles, first steps, first poop in the potty, give way to the exhilaration of watching your child's joy the first time he really connects bat to T-ball, or she beats you in Candy Land, or discovers ice cream, or gets paid for a job well done.

Daily family life becomes a series of debuts, an unfolding drama of opening night premiere performances that changes your thinking from yesteryear to the future. Prime time dads can joyfully dispense endless first time magic to their children while receiving its psychological benefits themselves.

Look, I played high school football in the trenches of the offensive and defensive lines, yet I was thoroughly enchanted when I bought the first baby doll of my life, at age 52, for my darling daughter.

I was accustomed to buying toys for her older brother, but I'd never before even looked at the doll sections of any of the toy stores. She so loved the dolls she played with at others' homes and pre-school, it finally came time she had one of her own.

I remember driving to the toy store with the usual thoughts about bills, work, and errands. But as soon as I exited the car and walked toward the store, I was filled with a magical feeling of embarking on a special adventure. I hurried along with an airy light skip in a positively-charged altered perceptive state.

I ventured for the first time ever into the doll section of our regular toy store. It was quieter there, pink and frilly, with startling little eyes peering out at me from every direction. This was different fun.

A mother with a toddler in tow eyed me suspiciously, and corralled her arm around her daughter. This was standard operating procedure when I was out in daylight during normal working hours. I'm a normal looking man, learned my manners, even had dinner in the White House. But place any man where mothers don't expect him to be during times when "he should be at work," and most ladies will transform into momma bears. I was careful not to knock anything over.

I studied the dolls, read their labels, and gravitated toward a selection from France that was simple and sweet, without the frills of whining, wetting, and winking. As I studied the box, the woman with a toddler apparently decided I was safe, and commented, "That's a lovely doll."

"Yes," I replied. "It's my daughter's first. I want it to be special." She smiled and assured me it was, which I'd already decided. I bought it, had the store wrap it, and I hurried home to present it to her.

"Surprise for my baby girl," I announced entering the house. She ran to me, but eyed me suspiciously until she knew this was not one of dad's tricks. "It's for you, honey." She tore into the wrapping paper and exploded with excitement when she saw the pretty pink doll.

It was hand-to-hand combat keeping her off the box while I untwisted the four thousand or so wires and plastic fasteners that kept it tidy inside its packaging, but finally, she hugged her new baby tightly to her chest, and jumped up and down with what I'd have to describe as pure joy.

My heart swelled. Such a simple act provided such happiness. This was her very own first baby doll, and she loved it unconditionally right out of the box. Just as I did her.

Prime time dads can joyfully dispense endless first time magic to their children while vicariously receiving its psychologically beneficial "first" aid themselves. You'll be feeling the healing the first time your youngster says, "I love you, daddy."

When our daughter was in second grade, many years after this doll joined our family, she pondered what to take for her turn at show and tell. She decided all on her own to show "First Baby Doll," as it's always been affectionately known in our household.

TWENTY-FOUR

....

YOU'RE NOW A MORE
WILY COYOTE

You've witnessed, played, been bloodied by, and survived enough office politics, social shenanigans, and the three-card-Monte shuffling strife of life to know that the game does not always go to the best or the brightest. Oftentimes, it's the clever who pull the right lever to win the day. And as a mature dad, you'll be glad to have your years of seasoned resourcefulness on your side.

A trace of treachery, a card shark's sleight of hand, and the persuasive eloquence of a con man will help keep you ahead of the game, even when you're way out of bounds.

Here's an example. When my eager kids were young and my energy flagged, I created out of necessity this offshoot of the familiar game of hide of seek. I'd offer to be "it." I'd sink my back onto the sofa and count aloud up to 25 as the kids scattered to various rooms searching for hiding places.

After the counting, I'd periodically shout out phrases such as, "Well, no one's in the kitchen," and "Anyone in the office?" all the while enjoying the luxury of stolen moments of relaxation provided by the comfy couch. I'd stay in this position, pretending to search, until the kids grew impatient, got wise to me, and sought me out, or until my guilt got the better of me.

Another game I played was calisthenics, in which I'd be the coach on the couch commanding the kids to run through various exercises. The kids ran in place, did somersaults, deep knee bends, squat-thrusts, push-ups, sit-ups, hurdled over an inflated rubber bat, and anything else I could come up with, while I held up fingers scoring their performances like an Olympic judge. Hey, we all had fun, the kids got some exercise and tuckered out for bedtime, and good ol' Dad finessed a little more down time.

One last game. My wife often had Sunday morning obligations which left me alone for extended periods of time with my son and daughter. Before becoming a dad, Sunday mornings had been my catch-up-on-sleep time. But that was usurped by fatherhood's demands and the early-rising children now in my life. How was I to cope with my young ones on Sunday morning?

We started playing the fort game. I'd throw some blankets and sheets over chairs and a card table and build the biggest fort I could. Then I'd put on my favorite music, lie on my back inside the fort, and tell the kids to go out on patrol to find various toys and stuffed animals to man the fort.

I got hours of music-filled relaxation time as the kids scurried about looking for Elmo and Batman and their ilk, returned to set them up inside the fort, and then eagerly awaited new orders to go and find the next batch.

Delve deep into the devious parts of your mind. Tell your youngsters that getting their own drinks of water saves the rings of Saturn, or that going to bed on time ensures Santa's elves have the time to make toys, or that science has proven that playing outdoors actually improves the taste of ice cream.

Or tell them that taking out the trash builds character, doing homework grows brain cells, and helping dad with chores manufactures muscles. Wait a minute, that's all true.

As youngsters, my two brothers and I would wrestle with our father on the living room floor. We'd hold down Dad's arms while Paul, the youngest, would run from the other room, fly through the air, and pounce on his prominent belly.

One day, Dad just stopped playing this game. No more wrestling. We accepted his decision, but we didn't understand it until years later when he confessed that, "You guys got too strong. I really couldn't get up. I had to stop playing that game!"

Whatever you conjure up can work, and since you've been around the block a few times, I'll bet you're fairly adept at the "con" part of conjure.

My wife insists she does not know how to create the kinds of games I do to grab a few precious moments of extra relaxation. She claims to marvel at my cunning creativity. I just hope she doesn't figure out my scam about having to watch all the financial shows on TV in order to keep us financially secure, because that's when I try to catch a little nap.

TWENTY-FIVE

....

YOU'RE PRIMED FOR A
PRIMAL ADVENTURE

Since you're old enough to have lived through many adventures, finding new ones can be a bit problematic. As a mature man, you are probably less inclined to hang-glide over Mt. Kailua or take up extreme steel-octagon fighting.

Have you lost your love of adventure? No. If you're like me, your idea of fun has shifted. But don't despair. There still remains the most eye-opening, demanding and ultimately rewarding adventure trip yet to explore. It's not on the map; in fact, it's mostly in the mind. Next stop, Fatherhood Frontier.

Becoming a prime time dad will take you to a brand new world of unrepentant natural wildlife.

You may witness first hand and up close the vivid sights, chaos and indelible wonder of birth, and afterbirth.

Marvel at the endless coloration, texture, and aromatic variations of mammalian excrement as you analyze it for clues about health and diet and the cause of diapers leaking all over the sofa cushions.

Witness the family unit dreaming about the newborns' highest college and career trajectories while simultaneously sinking into the language deterioration of "goo-goo-gah-gah, baby wanna nah-nah?"

As a father, you will experience heretofore hidden sites and rare sights. Who knew there was so much stuff to explore in the sand underneath the park swing? Watch your head! "No, don't put that in your mouth!"

You'll search department stores for hours looking for the dark, never-before-used elevators that are safer for baby strollers than dangerous entangling escalators.

See the post-partum, sleep-deprived mother fall asleep strapped to a motorized breast-milking apparatus. Be sure to take her photograph. You may be able to trade the original for a night out with the boys.

No amusement park roller coaster or heart-stopping ride can match the terror you'll experience when you look up from your *Consumer Reports* article on jogging strollers to find that your child is no longer where you set her down with the melt-in-the-mouth mush crackers and sippy cup. (She's over by the tree looking at lady bugs.)

You'll enjoy the camaraderie of a host of new and fascinating travel companions that may include Elmo, any number of new princesses, Army soldiers, Spiderman, Pokémon characters, and every cuddly stuffed animal ever offered by those endlessly clever marketeers who strive to trade their colorful collections for your green.

Refine your ear to study new language and thought process development. When recently told she must split the last piece of pizza with her sibling, one of the young creatures in my household replied, "I'll take the top half," meaning the part with all the delicious toppings. Local loco logic like that makes perfect sense when you go native and stand in their mud tracks on the carpet.

There are endless video opportunities, exotic new foods to avoid at all costs, and dangers lurking at every cross street, stairway, medicine cabinet and non-baby-proofed building.

But for those mature men brave enough to take the first steps into the wilds of Fatherhood Frontier, it's truly the grandest adventure of them all.

TWENTY-SIX

....

FIND A NEW WORLD OF
ART

As a childless man, I paid little, if any, attention to the thriving world of art created for children. Sure, I knew there were children's sections in libraries, and that Disney still made movies, but I hadn't watched *The Wizard of Oz* in decades and hadn't thought about *Curious George* for even longer.

I figured children's art was essentially messaged with the same old homogenized homilies I'd seen as a kid. No need to return there for any reason.

Then I became a prime time dad and was thrown crashing through the looking glass to rediscover and reunite with the delightful world of magically wonderful, creative film, books, and theatre for kids. And, shiver me timbers, the books became more relevant and the flicks got better. What happened? Where'd I been?

As a parental mind-food gatekeeper, you must be discriminating, but much of kids' art and entertainment is excellent. Many of the most recent, most watched, largest grossing films, books and entertainment vehicles in the world are targeted for children and their parents.

Youngsters and parents alike become immersed in whimsical readings of *Where the Wild Things Are*, children's high-flying theatrical performances of *Peter Pan*, the graceful magnificence of *The Nutcracker*, the jazzy rhythms of Ella Jenkins, the increasingly fast releases of DVD children's film classics old and new from Disney and Pixar, and of course, *Harry Potter* everything, everywhere.

While most of children's television is loathsome, I promised my darling daughter that I'd publicly confess to enjoying *Good Luck Charlie*, the only well-written and funny television comedy on Disney Channel. I started as a viewer because my daughter wanted to watch it, so I pointed out how the writers weaved the three story lines together toward conclusion. Many months later, while mindlessly scanning the cable channels to see what was on, I discovered to my surprise that I was willing to watch *Good Luck Charlie* alone, without her by my side.

Both of our kids have performed on stage in children's theatrical productions put on by summer camps and outreach efforts from our local children's theatre. The kids practice their lines in the living room, pacing, fretting, sorting out the memory kinks, and demanding "silence while I work!" just like professional prima donnas.

At theatre camp they help construct and paint the sets, gather the costumes, sing the songs, dance, and rehearse. Show time finds them on stage in make-up, with us in the audience, cameras in hand and hiding the flowers and balloons we present to them after the show.

When it was my daughter's turn as "Star of the Week" in her second grade class (all the kids get this honor bestowed upon them at some point during the school year), one of the optional activities during the week was for a parent of the Star to visit the class to read a story. I'd read some Shel Silverstein to my son's class when he was the Star, so I asked if she'd like the same funny, wildly irreverent, rhyming ritual performed.

128

"No!" she insisted. She was the Star, and she wanted me to read *Cinder Edna*, which is written by Ellen Jackson and illustrated by Kevin O'Malley.

I pushed my point. "But, I don't know *Cinder Edna*, and it might not be right for the boys in the class." Guess who won the argument.

Cinder Edna is Cinderella's neighbor, but unlike Cinderella who wishes for a fairy godmother to help her out, Cinder Edna mows lawns to make enough money to afford her own dress and bus fare for the prince's ball. It's an absolutely delightful, funny story about girl power that raises modern counterpoints to Cinderella, and everyone, including all the boys, laughed at all the right moments during my reading.

Afterwards, I asked her how it was received. She beamed up at me smiling, "Perfect, dad, everyone loved it!" Most of all, her dad.

Here's my challenge to those of you considering becoming parents but who haven't seen a kid's film or play for years. Read the movie reviews, pick out a couple of good films, and go see them. Notice how the scripts work on many levels, with jokes for the kids and jokes over their heads meant for the parents accompanying them. Notice how packed the theater is, and how many adults are smiling and having fun.

See a couple of live performances at your local children's theater or school (these productions can always use your ticket-buying support). Notice that no one cares whether actors freeze or lines are flubbed or sets topple or costumes rip. It's a joyous, handclapping bravo celebration of the arts and life. If you don't come out smiling like the Cheshire Cat, you weren't paying attention.

- - - - - - - - - - - - - - -

New art can sometimes walk right into your living room. When our son was very young, about three, he loved watching animated movies that were set in Africa, resplendent with the colorful creatures of the wild.

One day while my wife and I were talking at home, we noticed something strange. It was quiet. We hadn't heard from our son for quite some time. Contrary to what non-parents might think, this type of silence is not golden. You see, with little ones, when you hear the noises from their play and constant questioning and demands, things are okay. When there's silence, it could mean trouble.

We called out to him, and he came running to us briskly, smiling happily, wearing only underpants. He had black lines inked all over his bare chest, face, arms and legs.

"I'm a zebra!" he exclaimed, proudly showing off his body canvas. He searched our faces for signs that the jungle party would soon begin, but I guess we were frowning. Poor guy. When he saw our concern, and we told him how dangerous ink in his blood could be, he began to cry. He didn't even have a chance to enjoy his transformation.

This was one those rare moments when I kept my cool. I got a washcloth, grabbed a slippery bottle of mineral oil from a medicine cabinet, put him in my lap, and gently, lovingly swabbed every line of ink off him. Lucy and I talked and laughed with him the entire time. It was tender and touching. The poor kid's skin was rubbed red and raw, but I guess that was part of the price he paid for his art.

- - - - - - - - - - - - - - -

On a recent family vacation to the Big Apple, we wanted to keep our kids connected to the arts and especially theatre. We purchased tickets to the musical *Jersey Boys*, and although some of the language was a bit salty for youngsters, the show was as fun, fast, and fervent as a twist party.

After about two songs, my son leaned over to me whispering with amazement, "Dad, the singers sound so good, I thought they were lip-synching. But they're really singing!"

I beamed. "This is Broadway, son."

Back home, I bought a best of The Four Seasons compact disc, and the kids request to hear it played loudly when we drive on extended car trips. We all relive the experience of *Jersey Boys*, and I also get to reminisce about Brylcreem pompadours, vanilla cokes, and teen scene jukeboxes.

TWENTY-SEVEN

....

HOLIDAY ROUTINE
COMES ALIVE

As you roll into the middle decades of your life, even your once favorite holidays can become routine and more of a chore than a cheer. Does your appetite vanish upon sight of your aunt's cranberry sauce, its slimy sides channeled by the aluminum can in which it's been embalmed for more years than you care to imagine?

Why put up a Christmas tree when no one's around to appreciate it and you'll be getting dry needles stuck in your socks all year?

Ever forget to buy candy and then turn out the porch lights so the little goblins won't trick or treat at your door?

Even getting away from it all loses much of its appeal when you face the hordes of travelers removing their shoes and belts in security lines, the overcrowded overhead baggage compartments, the surly flight attendants, and the sliver of ocean seen only by stretching your neck over the balcony railing in some high-priced hotel decked out in plastic holiday veneer.

Want to lose your holiday blues? Have children. It's almost as though a kid's very existence is attuned to some internal clock that ticks off the year's holidays. Once the Thanksgiving turkey carcass is out of the soup pan and into the garbage can, the Christmas decorations come out of storage.

I can't vouch for how much history our kids are soaking up from our discussions of the Fourth of July, Presidents Day, and Martin Luther King Day, but they sure like fireworks, hot dogs and a long weekend with no homework.

I had one birthday party growing up, and most of my friends had just one, too. Times have changed. Each of our kids, and it seems all their friends, has a major birthday party every single year. And the ante keeps going up. Parents dig deep into their cerebral and cash reserves to come up with better, more unique party ideas.

It's crazy, but once you became a dad, you'll probably jump in enthusiastically to lead the madness. The holiday joy on little faces is positively contagious. You'll host the hot dog roasts, carve pumpkins, saw down pine trees, shop for perfect presents and theme decorations, and spread the family joy that is really at the core of all these celebrations.

Halloween rivals all holidays for kid fun and eager anticipation, although any day without the usual constraints on excessive candy is a virtual holiday to children. As a single man, I'd pretty much given up on Halloween. The wild Halloween party days of excess and naked women wrapped in plastic wrap were over (alas). But like those carved "puking" pumpkins, Halloween became ever so hollow for me. Some years, I turned off the porch light, didn't answer the doorbell, and went to bed early. Boo, humbug!

But then came my children. They love anticipating Halloween's arrival, searching through the mail order catalogues, planning their costumes, trick or treating, spreading and categorizing their candy on the floor, and overdosing on it before we trade it in for books. This holiday that had lost all its appeal suddenly became as alive as walking dead zombies.

We now have a neighborhood Halloween party every year on our driveway. My wife makes her famous chili, and the kids and I spend hours spreading out our growing assortment of gravestone, coffin, skeleton, and witch paraphernalia that we've acquired over the years. After a bite to eat, the kids go forth in groups to do their best to acquire all the candy their young arms can carry. It's a blast.

Your children will experience holidays with fresh, shining, wonder-filled eyes, and you, like Scrooge after his ghostly visitations, will be forever transformed. You'll rediscover and relive anew the joyful essence of these celebrations. Now, stir up the fires and create another warm memory, "before you dot another i!"

- - - - - - - - - - - - - -

Thinking about holidays, here are a few parental milestones that should be celebrated as vigorously as a 21st birthday falling on New Year's Eve.

Diaper Independence Day

OMG, when junior finally learns to poop and pee in the toilet, your blood pressure and heart rate will reduce dramatically because you'll no longer have to tax your entire mind, will, and essential life force trying to come up with reasonable-sounding excuses why you can't change him this time.

Seatbelt Click It Day

Doesn't sound like such a big deal does it? But you'll pop the sparkling cider when the youngsters finally learn to fasten their own seat belts, relieving you of the bent-over, back breaking, time-stopped-ticking burden.

Tie Their Own Shoes Day

Tying your kids' shoelaces is lumbar numbing labor, and untangling the knots they weave is Gordian torture. And this parental finger fumbling can go on for years because so many shoes are now secured with Velcro fasteners. Today's children may not learn to tie their own shoes until the fifth grade. Go ahead, confirm this with others parents if you don't believe me.

Safely Get Their Own Drinks Day

I used to celebrate "Get Their Own Drinks Day," but learned this was premature and added the word "safely" after wiping up scores of spills on the floor, inside the refrigerator, and over the utensils. Anyone out there remember the movie *The Graduate*? I just want to say one word to you. Just one word (well maybe three). Are you listening? Plastics – drinking cups.

Back to School Day

A word to the wise, this is a half-day celebration. The sense of freedom, the daydreaming about accomplishing all those set-aside projects, the enticing visions of catching up with friends, grabbing a leisurely latte, perchance to nap, all come crashing down to Earth as the young scholars burst back through the front door early in the afternoon. "Hey Dad, I think I left my photo day form on the playground."

I'm a regular blogger for *Huffington Post Parents* (http://www.huffingtonpost.com/len-filppu), and when I asked readers to send in their own special parental milestone holidays, I received numerous examples including: when kids finally sleep in their own beds, when they're old enough for drop-off play dates and parties, when they can take their own baths, when they can get themselves to and from school alone, when they can wrap presents by themselves, when they can safely swim, when they can hang out with friends on the weekends, and when they can ride a bike around town without needing a lift, among others. Thank you to all who submitted these gems, and for all of you parents and those thinking about parenthood, Happy Holidays!

TWENTY-EIGHT

··

YOU'RE A BETTER MULTI-TASKING PROBLEM SOLVER

If I need a job done that requires simultaneous focus and effort across multiple fronts, I'll choose a mature man over a younger man any day of the week. Why? Because they know how to get the job done.

We've lived longer so we have more experience. We've already learned from measuring once and sawing thrice. As the wise old farmer said, "Good judgment comes from experience, and a lotta that comes from bad judgment."

You, as a mature man, likely have gained more diverse skills, and are not so easily distracted. You're more experienced at seeing the big picture, juggling many balls at the same time, pushing complex projects through to the finish, under-standing and managing the many pieces that make up the whole, and seeking and implementing the advice of experts when you need it. These traits are indispensable to anyone who becomes a father.

When my son was about three, he stated loudly between simultaneous demands for more milk, his toys and candy, that "I wish Mommy was an octo-pus!" When asked why, he answered with perfect kid logic that if Mommy had eight arms, she could more easily get all her tasks done and still help him with his needs.

This moment has provided us many chuckles over the years, probably because of the truth at its core. Parents must be adept at multi-tasking or their two arms will be wrapped tight in a straight jacket on a ride to the funny farm. I argue that prime time dads have the advantage of experience over younger guys.

If you're a childless man, you may find it hard to imagine that taking a simple vacation involving air transportation with small children becomes a major event requiring the advanced thinking and logisti-cal planning of a military invasion.

For example, given that you've found a week on your schedule that does not require you or your spouse to meet work deadlines or your kids to have vaccinations, you'll still need to deal with car seats for the ride to the airport and wherever you land, diaper bags, more pieces of luggage, strollers, identity verification for the children, snack food, toys and trinkets to occupy them on the flight, and medicines and first aid items, among others.

Reserve your seats far enough in advance to ensure the family sits together, and arrive at the airport much earlier than recommended because juggling all this travel trove through security can be a nightmare.

Don't relax on the flight. You must figure out how to keep your kids from spilling milk on, or pulling the hair of, the passengers in front of you, and you've got to plan ahead on how you intend to get all your stuff from the baggage claim into the car rental bus and onto the minivan. You did remember to rent a minivan, didn't you?

This is just one little example of how your life will become more complicated with the addition of children. It's all doable and fun, well worth the effort, and there are legions of trained experts to help. I highly recommend the juggling joys of parenthood.

The leadership, problem-solving, and management skills you've acquired through your longer lifetime meeting and matching your fair share of projects will come in most handy, even if you have only two hands.

- - - - - - - - - - - - - - -

For years now, whenever the kids go off to school or I go off on some business, I've made it a point to tell them, "I love you." My daughter and I have hand signals to communicate this. We touch our eye, then our heart, then point at one another and blow a kiss. I can send her this silent message as she's preparing to swim a race or go on stage or when she's reading comfortably on the couch.

But the kids are getting a bit older now. The outside world is leaking in. They are learning and hearing about and sometimes observing issues such as bullying, sex, eating disorders, drugs and alcohol use, and even suicide.

I've changed my farewell slogan. When they head off to school now, instead of saying "I love you," I say, "Remember, we can find a solution to any problem."

TWENTY-NINE

....

REDISCOVER YOUR PARENTS

As I grew up and watched the years carve their passage onto the landscape of my parents' faces, I figured that I'd really gotten to know them, that I understood who they were and what made them tick. Wrong.

My truth is, until you have your own children, you cannot really understand your parents. It's just a fact of life. It stems from traveling the same journey wearing the same shoes, although decades apart.

When you become a dad, you'll mentally climb into the same foxhole your folks occupied. The invisible veil that cloaked your parents' inner lives, motivations and actions falls away. You'll understand them with new insight and appreciation, and smilingly reacquaint yourself with them as you would dear friends not seen in decades.

It's an almost daily occurrence that some aspect of my parental life triggers a half-forgotten memory of my parents. For instance, my father let me defeat him at chess before I really understood how the pieces moved. I remember being thrilled, not yet understanding his enticing strategy, and this victory encouraged me to learn the game early and to partake in other games and competitions.

I remember waking up on my eighth birthday to discover that my mom had forgotten to bake a treat for my third grade party celebration at school. I was crestfallen. Frantic with the morning madness of getting her brood up, fed, dressed, and out the door with full Robin Hood lunchboxes, she nevertheless swung into action to bake my cupcakes. I marvel at how hard she worked and sacrificed for us, how much she loved us.

Almost every night, I tell my children, "Night, night, sleep tight, don't let the bed bugs bite," just as I'd heard growing up. And on every first day of school, I do my best trying to sing to my kids a re-membered rendition of "School days, school days, good ol' golden rule days."

These small, tender, reacquainting reminiscences of my parents as parents flood my mind regularly, inspired by ordinary daily interactions with my own children. It's the shared universality of parental love that bonds us tighter, so many years apart.

This ability to re-examine and appreciate my folks anew is a special surprise bonus of fatherhood. My mother and father are no longer alive, yet they regularly reach out and vividly connect with me through my interactions with my kids.

When I was a child, my father tricked me into eating sharp cheddar cheese by calling it "man's cheese." Wanting to be a man and be like my dad, I gobbled it up. I had no idea cheddar cheese had its own name until I asked for it by the man's cheese moniker in the grade school cafeteria. The confusion on the cafeteria ladies' faces, followed by laughter when they understood, taught me my father's ruse. Man's cheese is a hit in our home today, serving up protein and fond memories with every savory chunk.

And the first time I taught my son chess, he won.

- - - - - - - - - - - - - - -

As a prime time man, you have a better opportunity to avoid your parents' mistakes. Time has provided you with the distance to view your own childhood from a keener, more objective perspective. Sure, your parents made errors raising you. All parents do. You will, too.

Chances are your parents were probably young parents. As such, they may have been less well prepared to deal with the challenge of children. You, with more mature eyes, can now see the pros and cons of your upbringing more clearly. You're better equipped to avoid the mistakes that send some to psychotherapy for years.

Did you ever tell your parents the truth and not be believed? Were you so rigidly controlled in childhood that you exploded with self-destructive behavior at the first taste of freedom? Can you believe the frozen TV dinners that passed for food back then?

All of us have issues with the way we were raised. Because you are now more distanced from the immediacy of the maelstrom, you can see more clearly. Having children a bit later in life gives you the chance to right some wrongs, break bad cycles, and even come to terms with and fix the past.

Those who are too close to their own history have less of a chance of understanding and learning from it.

My dad was a veteran of World War II. He did the best he could, was a loving and thoughtful father, but he sure made what I'd consider to be "mistakes." It's strange, but even though we playfully wrestled and engaged in much physical activity through sports, I cannot remember a single time my father hugged me and kissed me.

Back in the dark dawn of time that was 1950s America, fathers were customarily colder, less apt to display their emotional sides. I remember watching the Italian dad of a close friend of mine hugging and kissing him. While my friend often squirmed from his dad's embrace, I could tell he enjoyed this demonstration of affection. I was secretly envious.

So, while I'm not labeling my own dad's more rigid approach an official mistake, I will tell you in no uncertain terms that my own children get an almost daily application of sloppy kisses, hugs for no reasons, and pronouncements of my unconditional love for them. The parental pendulum has swung.

Here's another example: When I was about 15 years old, my father said he wanted to show me something. He led me upstairs into his bedroom, opened the top drawer of his dresser, and lifted up a pile of handkerchiefs to reveal a box of condoms.

I still remember the brand, Ramses. I guess the manufacturer of Ramses wanted another image from antiquity to compete with Trojans. But the Egyptian king Ramses reportedly fathered 160 children, so it's little wonder why this brand has been discontinued.

Anyway, Dad said, "Here are the safes. I'm going to tell you what Dr. Jones told his kids." Dr. Jones, not the real name of my dad's colleague professor at the local college, had a brood of rough and tumble boys.

"If you get a girl pregnant," my dad continued, "don't bother coming home." With that, he left the room. That was it. That was his drive-by, hit-and-run method of sex education. And he was an educated man, a university professor of economics. And "safes," don't you love that term? Never heard it used before or since.

Hanging on to that swinging parental pendulum for dear life, I took my boy to a father-son sex education class at our local hospital when he was 11. My wife had signed us up. She was almost giddy from the program's great reviews heard through her ever-flowing moms' grapevine. "Everyone says it's the best. You'll love it," she exclaimed. Of course, she wasn't going.

I silently dreaded the reality of a graphic immersion into the world of human sexuality with my offspring without the props of a punch line or locker room towel snap. Yet daddy duty called, and as a father who strives to be aware and there, I certainly endorsed the concept of a truthful discussion about the challenges of puberty, sexuality, reproduction and the like.

Driving– slowly– to the appointment with my son, I wondered why I felt so apprehensive. Remembering my own father's dilemma about this subject and his curt "don't bother coming home" commandment made me smile with deeper understanding and empathy.

I watched as fathers and their sons entered the auditorium for the evening's edification. Each pair sat side by side, talking to one another in hushed voices, as if waiting for a funeral to commence. I quelled my tension by trying to place myself in my son's situation. Surely he must be feeling weirder than I was about being dragged to yet another event "that's good for him." I was careful not to squirm.

The lesson began, and I learned the true value of a good ice breaker. Having sat through innumerable meetings in which well-intentioned facilitators asked everyone to "go around the room and say something about themselves," I had my doubts.

But this was different. Our sex education teacher asked all the men to give a different synonym, however crude, for the penis. And he went around the room, got right up and into the faces of all the dads, and politely but firmly demanded that we come up with an answer, a different name each time.

It was hysterical. There were almost no repeats from about 60 dads. Cultural and geographic differences unearthed endless variety. Everyone, all the kids and dads, were laughing and loosening up, releasing fear and anxiety, and sharing in the common bodily bond of masculinity.

From there it was a breeze. On the way home, my son asked me a couple clarifying questions, and I was struck both by how basic are the knowledge needs of tweens and by how casually I was able to answer him. He was more like my sports buddy when I shared my information. I was not hung up by embarrassment or thoughts about what a proper dad might say. I just told him the truth in my own salty terms. My son listened intently, then said, "I get it."

And I got it. This sex education class transformed the taboo into the prosaic. It was the learning ladder that assisted our leap over a tricky hurdle. We connected more as fellow males rather than as father and son. And I'm confident this unspoken yet powerful linkage will help us confront future issues more forthrightly and solve them more readily. My fingers are crossed that this is true. I'm glad I didn't flunk out on my chance to go to sex ed class with my son.

As a prime time man with the maturity and perspective time provides, one can more clearly recognize and understand some of one's own parents' mistakes, and so armed, can choose to act to avoid repeating them. That's a good thing, because you'll make enough brand new ones of your own.

THIRTY

....

YOU KNOW YOURSELF
BETTER

Lao-Tzu, the father of Taoism, is credited with the quote, "Knowing others is intelligence; knowing yourself is true wisdom." To truly understand, appreciate, and help others, one must first know oneself. It's problematic to enhance the life of offspring if you are running around unsure of who you are and how you fit into the larger world.

We midlife men know ourselves better. As I've pointed out often, we've lived longer, and we've faced up, failed, and been feted more often. A greater body of life experience has taught us our capabilities and limitations, exposed our strengths and our weaknesses.

A few of us may actually read and heed the cautionary warning sign before walking out onto thin ice.

We are more comfortable with ourselves as mature men. Consistency is on our side. We stand for some things and no longer rise or fall for others. And even if true north keeps wandering, we are more apt to have developed a steadier moral compass.

More and more of our journey is inward, personal, spiritual. We know with more certainty that life does end, and this knowledge allows us to value more deeply the opportunity fatherhood gives us to spend time with our children.

When I first became a dad, I wanted to transmit to my offspring every possible skill, fact, and strategy about living. I was going to teach my kids how to paint a fence and fence with foils, dig for knowledge and earthworms, run in the wind and run for office, and how to pray and not be prey.

I started out like a whirling dervish, grandiose visions of father-child perfection driving me faster and farther, but I wound up overcommitted, in over my head, and dizzy.

Then my mature self intervened. I realized deep down inside that I couldn't teach them everything, and that the wiser path was to let the coaches, teachers, and Cub Scout leaders impart their knowledge while I focused on the things I really knew, few as they are.

So my daughter did not learn her beautiful butterfly stroke from me, and I did not teach my son how to ice skate. But I taught her card strategy, and he learned how to direct and shoot a home movie with me.

These are just a couple of examples, but I hope they make the point. I'm mature enough to know myself and to accurately assess what I actually bring to the party. I'm happy to let other experts fill in the gaps, gaping as they are in my case.

On the larger issues, I'm doing my best to see that my children are exposed to a dad who does what he says he will, treats others as he'd like to be treated, freely gives of his time and skills to the larger community, and curses only when the Cleveland Browns are losing (it's been a bit of a blue streak decade for the kids' tender ears).

Honestly, having children helps me remember to act out these more noble traits. I know they're watching, and I want them to see a decent role model. When I'm faced with the choice of an easier way or a tougher but right way, my inner director sternly reminds me that my audience is wide eyed and wide awake, and whatever it is I show, they will know.

And so, what goes around, comes around. I hope to make my kids better people, and in so doing, my kids make me a better person. One hand washes the other.

Knowing yourself well allows you to give genuinely and consistently of yourself. It is a great gift to bestow upon offspring to look them in the eye, day after day, year after year, and have them know the same person is really there, and is really there for them.

THIRTY-ONE

....

CREATE A NEW FAMILY HISTORY WITH NEW MEMORIES

Haven't you lived with your family of origin's history long enough? Each of us is born into a family that created its own unique history, lore, and rituals. We did not choose these fellow passengers. They are accidents of birth.

Whether it's the way your family gathered for dinner, chose up sides in touch football games, took vacations, celebrated holidays, shared the bathroom or the ice cream, you've lived all your life with this same shared family history in all its glory and gore.

Because you were a youngster, this history was essentially written for you, not by you. And frankly, they probably got many of the facts wrong.

As a prime time dad, you'll be able to create a new, unique ancestral anthology written specifically for your new nuclear family.

Why continue to be shackled by the rusting chains of past family ritual? Do you still mumble, "This place is saved," when you get up from the best TV viewing chair for a bathroom break, even if no one else is around?

Aren't you weary of the exaggerated self-serving claptrap some of your clan bloviate endlessly to put you down or them up?

And while your wife hates tinsel on the Christmas tree, don't you feel the holiday season is just not complete without spreading it on in clumsy clumps like in those chilly days of yore?

Our past family habits and lore are deeply embedded in our adult consciousness. What a rush of freedom and endless possibility fills our souls when we have our own children and realize we can now consciously create our own new mythology.

When we first had kids, my wife insisted we spend both the Thanksgiving and Christmas holidays visiting with her family in Southern California. They're lovely people, there's plenty to do, and that was fine, up to a point.

It dawned on me after several years of bumper to bumper traffic through California's Central Valley that our son and daughter were actually reliving my wife's past holiday experiences. I argued that we should create new and fresh holiday memories for our children, in and around their own home.

While we still head down south for New Year's Day and the Tournament of Roses Parade, we now enjoy our own memory-inducing Thanksgiving and Christmas here, in our home environs, creating our own history, lumpy gravy and all.

A few years ago, as Halloween approached, my daughter asked me what kinds of candies I had enjoyed as a child. She's also asked me if there were cars when I was a kid, so before dismissing her question by answering that we had Snickers and M&Ms and peanut butter cups just like today, I reflected back on some of those candies we had in the grey mists before time. I told her about Sky Bars, Mallo Cups, Turkish Taffy, and Mars Bars, candies I've not seen or heard about in decades.

She wondered aloud that, if they were such good candies, why weren't they still available? Great question, hers, which got me thinking. I web-searched these candies the next morning, and found an old time candy store that has stayed in touch with the manufacturers of some of those nostalgic candies and sells them online.

I ordered a bunch of Sky Bars, Mallo Cups, Turkish Taffy, bull's eye caramels, Nik-L-Nip drinks in wax bottles, Sno Caps, Bit-O-Honey, and Sugar Daddies. I told my kids these treats were coming, got them excited about the project, was outside playing with them when the delivery truck pulled up with the package, and created some sweet new family history for my kids based on the past.

When you become a father, at any age, you are no longer a bit player in your parents' play but the director of your own creation. You get to write and edit the script. By having kids, you will deeply en-joy the nostalgic remembrance of your past family lore, yet revel in the creation of your own uniquely branded version.

Just remember, while your histories may not repeat themselves, they'll probably rhyme, so add a wistful whistling score that keeps them both in time.

- - - - - - - - - - - - - - -

All of us have unpleasant memories that can toss us in the night and re-ignite from seemingly nowhere a flare of anger, a flush of buried embarrassment, the stab of betrayal, the draining sadness of loss.

Since becoming a prime time dad, I've noticed that these entrenched remnants of earlier negative feelings are getting crowded out by the more happy memories of my new life with children.

Fatherhood is making jolly some of my former melancholy. Perhaps with the flood of fatherhood experiences flowing into my head, there's simply no room left in the noggin to store past ill-understood embarrassments and insults.

But I think it's really about the insightful perspective parenthood provides. We all were hurt early in our lives. We didn't completely understand what was going on. We reacted as children, with childish emotions, and did childish things.

Now that I have children, I get to see how my actions impact them. I get to witness their childish reactions, their kid logic, their sensitivities and fears. And in the process, I better understand how faulty and misplaced and inappropriate and un-healthy were some of my own responses to early emotional bumps and bruises. I'm gaining a paren-tal perspective that helps heal.

When you have children, there'll be no need to romantically exaggerate or regret the memory of your election to class president or your selection as class clown. Instead, those experiences become op-portunities to pass along to your children some of the wisdom you've learned from your parental per-spective.

You'll be storing unique original life lore on a daily basis, the raw material to create new memo-ries, new history, that will delight and enrich your family and your life.

THIRTY-TWO

....

YOU CAN STILL BECOME
A HERO

I remember my childhood dreams of becoming an NFL football star, saving someone's life as a Boy Scout, exploring the seas as a famous aquanaut. Time and reality whittle away at these heroic daydreams.

Fate and character choose only a few larger than life heroes. They're found on the battlefields, disaster zones, city buses, and in classrooms throughout world. They inform and inspire us by their acts of courageous selflessness. As mere mortal men, we may have missed the boat to become historical figures. But there are endless opportunities to serve as everyday heroes.

Everyday heroes exhaustedly crawl out of bed to earn a living for their families. They leave their TV ballgame or nap or work to answer the requests of their children to play or look at a butterfly or wipe a behind or pour milk.

Everyday heroes extract slivers from feet, hold their feverish and coughing offspring all night long, take time to answer endless questions about how this works or how that's made. They put aside adult things to embrace childish things. Everyday heroes hold the line, their anger, the stinking diaper bag, and an enormously warm place in their kids' hearts.

Sure, everyday heroes know their acts of giving, teaching, caring, husbandry, and self-sacrifice are prosaic parental procedures performed since cave dwelling days. But everyday heroes aren't looking for medals or acclaim.

They nod and smile encouragingly to other everyday hero parents, helping them keep the balance. They keep toiling in the face of seemingly insurmountable obstacles because of the all-encompassing, elemental love unveiled through parenthood, and for that occasional, sincere look of total admiration from the toddler whose favorite toy's been magically fixed by the everyday hero's simple changing of the batteries.

It's invariably the simple things that make heroes of parents. My daughter has always loved watching *Cake Boss*, the television show about the New Jersey bakery that creates truly artistic cakes for various celebrations. Every time we watched the show together, she determinedly said, "I want to go that bakery."

Well, last summer we went to visit New York City, and we decided to make one of our day outings a trip to Hoboken to see Carlo's Bakery, home of *Cake Boss*. Yes, we waited in line considerably longer than a New York minute, but our daughter was thrilled with the subway and train rides, the bakery's delicious lobster tails, and the fact that this adventure was customized to fulfill her dream.

When my son was in first or second grade, he presented me with a large handmade card featuring a colorful portrait of a smiling man with short, thinning hair, obviously yours truly. It's still up on the wall in my office. The card reads: "My hero is my dad. He taught me a magic trick. He gets in very good shape. He is a great dad."

Section IV.

Savoring the Burn

THIRTY-THREE

....

FATHERHOOD'S A GREAT REASON TO STAY IN SHAPE

Having kids can provide you the motivation you may need to get in and stay in shape. When you look into your son's bright eyes after he says, "You shouldn't eat french fries, Daddy, they're no good for you," rather than get upset at your spouse for planting this nutritional notion in his head, you may realize that everyone actually really does want you to stay around for the long run.

Unless you're a fitness devotee, a marathoner, or offspring of Olympian athletes, you may have developed a bit of a spare tire around your belly over the years. You may have slid into "a body at rest tends to stay at rest" non-exercise inertia that's not conducive to running up the stairs at work without straining your heart and lungs. Relax, it happens to most of us. Beware though, it's a downward slide that can restrict your activities and shorten your life.

We've all enrolled at the gym in January or started a personal exercise program fully determined that this time we'd stick with it. But staying the course is tough. Exercise partners' schedules change, that movie you've seen twenty times is on TV again, microwave popcorn screams for you to answer its imitation-buttery siren's song, and you can always hit the gym tomorrow or the day after, if you finish that rush project at work.

As you pound out the first steps on a short walk or jog, fill your heart and mind with the knowledge that you have real, living, breathing human beings who need you, are cheering for you, and counting on you every agonizing, knee-twinging step of the way. You can do it, especially when your motivation is the product of your procreation.

I recently cut way back on eating sugar. No, I haven't gone for a highfalutin, non-pollutin', can't-eat-gluten, Hollywood diet fad. I'm not gnawing on pine bark, and I still enjoy occasional white pastas, bread, and pizza crust.

But my six-pack had transformed over the years into a frat-party-sized kegger, and my doctor didn't sugar coat it when he told me in no uncertain terms that sugar is a killer that can reduce life expectancy by 12 years.

That's exactly what I needed to hear. I cut way down on ice cream, candy, pastries, and anything else with mountains of refined sugar. For those of you paying attention, I did eat some of the old-time nostalgic candy discussed earlier, couldn't resist it, but it was then back to the sugar boycott and the gym.

I lost double-digit pounds without really dieting or trying. That weight loss is probably a testament to the unhealthy amounts sugar I was consuming. My head got clearer, I had more energy, natural foods tasted better and I craved them, and I was inspired to work out more.

Over the years, I've yo-yoed a few times with eliminating sugar and carloads of white flour-based carbs from my diet, and when I succumb to the sweets, I quickly add back the pounds. Sugar is addictive. For me, it's either a screaming monkey on my back or it's safely in a cage where I give it a knowing nod while passing by.

Hard as it is to initiate and maintain new healthy habits, it's never too late to tinker with fitness. Even those of you who are physically fit will benefit from ongoing health-conscious vigilance and variety. I'm amazed at how our bodies can bounce back and respond positively to the simple joys of regular exercise and smart choices of food.

The human body is remarkably resilient, and the human spirit is firmly attached to it. When I've gotten fed up with how I've ill fed my body and decided to eat better and exercise, I quickly shed some pounds, sleep better, increase my muscle mass through weightlifting, and feel not just physically fit but also more mentally alert and eager to face the day's challenges.

My joy of life rises with each extra mile on the elliptical and choice of fruit bar over ice cream bar. My natural animal spirit is energized, re-awakened. My mood may not hit full roar, but it doesn't stay in dull snore.

A few years ago, I went into the cupboard for a fix of potato chips, a snack food that continues to bedevil and beckon me. I found a note from my son on top of the bag. It read: "No chips, Dad! You'll gain pounds. Unhealthy." His notes have an impact on me.

Above all other influences, be they self-image, athletic, sex appeal or getting practical use out of the smaller-waist trousers hanging in the closet, becoming a father has motivated me the most to get back in shape. I want to stay around to help and enjoy my children. And believe me, since I used to push plates with Methuselah, if I can do it, so can you.

THIRTY-FOUR

....

COACH YOUR FAVORITE
SPORT(S)

As the years have gone by, maybe you've grown closer to your old couch than your old coach. But having kids will give you the chance to live out your latent, lingering Paul Brown, Bill Walsh, or Jon Gruden fantasies.

Never a star athlete? It doesn't matter. Forgot the rules? No problem. Haven't thrown a ball for decades? You're in. Think you can dribble a football? Alright, timeout, we've got an issue there.

Coaching youngsters' sports teams is not about athletic skill, game knowledge, or advanced strategy. It's mainly a matter of showing up and stepping up. Anyone can do it.

Kids love to play physical sport games, but whether its soccer or T-ball or basketball, until a certain age – around six – they really can't follow the rules or comprehend the team part of team-work. They tend to leave their positions to chase the soccer ball as a group. They dribble to the middle of the court and then sit down protecting the basketball. They hit a T-ball line drive into short center and run off to third base while the outfielders look for four-leafed clovers. It's a riot.

Here's what you need to do to get the coach's shirt for your kid's team (and the cliché is based on reality). Show up early to the first session and when they ask for volunteers, simply stand still as everyone else sheepishly inches backwards. Thanks, coach, here's your shirt. Have a ball.

- - - - - - - - - - - - - -

While on the subject of sports, here's an observation about parenthood that'll make sense to you basketball fans out there.

As mentioned often in these pages, I had rookie nervousness about becoming a later in life father, but after my wife and I worked through evolving strategies and techniques, our heads got in the game. Sure there were dropped passes, personal and technical fouls, and plenty of missed shots, but all in all, our team was holding its own, and we belonged on the court.

So when Lucy suggested we have another child, I thought, "You know, she really wants another baby, the kids would have a sibling, and this fatherhood thing is not as bad as I thought. Okay, let's go for it."

We had our baby girl, and in a clock tick, our game changed from a methodical but leisurely zone defense to an exhausting man-to-man full court press. Funny thing is, I never saw it coming. I was lulled by the easy nature of covering my own area of the court. You see, with one child, I could still go to the movies when Lucy watched him. She could have lunch with her girlfriends while I took him to the park. We each had a bit of free time sans child to do some of things we wanted.

But when you have two children, you're always on. Both parents have their hands full, the kids require different levels of simultaneous attention, eating, napping, and sleeping patterns are not synched up, and the only break comes at the end of day when everyone's asleep and the parents collapse onto the mattress.

It's now so obvious to me that the parental workload grows exponentially from one child to two, that I'm amazed I didn't see it earlier. Nature must be adept at hiding pitfalls in order to evolve. Put another way, boy, was I dumb.

But the truth is, moving from a zone to a man-to-man defense has helped me get in much better condition to meet the toughest opposition and to become a fully committed, full time starter for the most important team on which I have ever had the honor of playing.

- - - - - - - - - - - - - - -

You may have noticed by this chapter that I'm a basketball fan. As a child in western New York winters, we'd work for hours scraping inch-thick ice off our backyard blacktop to play hoops for a few minutes.

But enough nostalgia, now on to a quick halftime attempt at hardwood humor. College basketball's March Madness offers parents a double bonus situation: excitement and insight. Behind the blitzkrieg of b-balling, beer commercials, and alumni boosterism, I found some parental tricks easily transferable from the polished courts to the stained-forever carpets of our cozy family room.

Jump Ball

This is so elegantly simple, I'm astonished not to have read about it somewhere in the cargo container load of parenting self-help literature strewn about our bedroom. If you have two or more kids who are fighting over the same thing– a toy, the last cupcake, the dog– throw it up in the air. The one who catches it, gets it. It's fair because the smaller children may be quicker or closer to the object of desire. And it may convince the dog to play outside once in a while.

Sweet Sixteen

My then nine-year-old daughter described, out of the blue, paragraphs upon pages of lovely details she wanted for her Sweet Sixteen birthday party, inspired, no doubt, by viewing television shows about baking cakes and cupcakes for parties. Sure, I loved her creativity, but my mind's eye kept attaching price tags to her dreams. Now I have the perfect retort. "Oh, Angel, don't you know– Sweet Sixteen is strictly a basketball term. It doesn't really apply to life."

Bracketology

The process of predicting winners for each game from the field of 68 teams through to the final champion is a simpler and quaintly more rudimentary form of what parents do every year when planning their summer breaks. Summertime calculations require parents to research, select, and juggle the right camps at the right times for each child, integrate educational, athletic, and musical training, choose not-yet-visited vacation destinations within budget, strategize adult work schedules, and shoehorn in that mandatory visit to the in-laws. This rigorous training puts parents in the money for the relatively easy and straightforward office bracketology contest.

Give Me the Ball

Basketball clearly shows us that, contrary to what every parent tells their offspring, giving does not mean you shall receive. It's a real life lesson every kid learns in the sand box. When you share your shovel and pail with a bigger kid, you may not get them back. Despite the alleged attention paid to basketball assist stats, the shooters get the glory. And when you pass to the shooting guards, power forwards and centers, don't expect to get the ball back. If you want to teach the valuable rewards of unselfish behavior, you better be raising a point guard.

A Little Money Goes a Long Way

Okay, I hope the FBI isn't reading this, but I enjoy a March Madness pool with some friends. The entry fee is a whopping $10. Curiously, that little bit of action makes me inordinately interested in the outcomes of all the games. Perhaps the same principle can be applied to some aspects of parenting. "Hey, Junior, if you bring home straight As on your report card, you can earn a few extra bucks." I've heard of this happening. Really. But if my wife and I ever stooped to such bribery, we'd have to consider it an advance payment on college tuition.

THIRTY-FIVE

....

YOU'VE OVERCOME MOST OF YOUR BAD HABITS

Since you're reading this, you're still alive. Many are not. They taunted safety and lost, they couldn't or wouldn't find the help available to understand and recover from addictions, or the grim reaper just picked their unlucky numbers.

But since you're still breathing air on this side of the grass, there's a good chance you may have quit smoking, cut down on booze intake, declined invites to rave parties, and in general have grown up enough to treat yourself to a more mature life devoid of some of the excessive bad habits of youth.

Congratulations. Your healthful, non-self-destructive lifestyle is most conducive to the nurturing of living things such as children. Kids watch parents with "magnet" eyesight; they're "attracted" to what they see. They do not do as they're told, but as they see. If you smoke, drink, curse, overeat, rage, lie, rob banks or rip the tags off mattresses, they'll notice it and chances are, they'll emulate it.

These early lessons can become psychologically entrenched burdens your children must overcome throughout their later lives. It's better to give them a lighter load of troubles to carry around.

Look, I'm no saint. But I try to make progress. I come from a radical 1960s background of political activism, living in a hippie commune-like environment, experimenting with all kinds of consciousness modifying activities, getting caught up in the trap of a party-fueled lifestyle, and finally coming out of the purple haze with a much clearer-eyed approach to life.

I'll bet some of you mature men reading this understand to some degree what I'm talking about. It just becomes physically impossible to keep up the pace we pounded out when young.

The fewer bad habits you model, the better for your children. My kids know I don't drink, don't do drugs, and don't smoke. They know I work out, try to stay in shape, and have altered my diet in an effort to become healthier. They encourage me in my efforts. They want me stay around, and I want to stay around to be there for them.

Tragedy struck our extended family earlier this year. My wife's sister's husband died suddenly from a massive stroke. He was not yet 60 years old. Besides his wife, he left behind his son, our children's cousin, who recently turned 15.

When my daughter began talking about this cousin's birthday, she started crying almost uncontrollably and inconsolably. She is a sensitive soul, wise beyond her pre-teen years in the ways of the human heart. She shed tears for how she imagined her cousin felt on his first birthday without his beloved father.

"It must be so painful," she howled, huge teardrops dripping down her reddened face. My wife hugged and talked with her, but she kept crying.

I monitored the storm from my office, waiting for the right moment. She eventually came to me, weeping wildly, brow creased, eyes searching for answers, perplexed by life's most visceral reality: death.

I took her in my arms and wiped her cheeks. I reminded her of our previous conversations about this baffling subject. I told her again how I've lost several loved ones, how I felt and thought about it, and how I found that life has ways of moving us on, positively.

She listened intently. The storm calmed. She looked deeply into my eyes, and with a voice I knew she was courageously commanding up from soul depth, she asked me, "You're not... you're not going... anywhere, are you?"

This was, of course, at the heart of it. I almost went into auto response mode by saying that everyone eventually dies, but I quickly caught myself. My baby needed a safe harbor.

"No, Sweetheart," I soothed. "I'm not going anywhere." She snuggled deeper into my arms. After some comfort time had passed, I suggested she phone her cousin to wish him a Happy Birthday. She did. She got back into the positive flow of life. I vowed to myself to continue my healthful ways.

My children watch me. They've made a habit of noticing my bad habits. They know when I binge on ice cream and when I choose salads, when I work out and when I blow off the gym. I still have some bad habits, but they're fewer than ever before. With my loving children as referees, I'm going to keep playing as clean a game as possible for as long as I can.

THIRTY-SIX

....

YOUR RUT IS ALREADY
FULLY DECORATED

Our life paths gouge out ruts in which we live and labor, and the older we get, the deeper and more comfortable these ruts can become. We live routinely inside their walls, decorate them fully, enjoy their safety and familiarity, and often neglect to climb up and out to see the real horizon.

There's nothing wrong with your favorite rut, unless of course, you sense it's become monotonous and unsatisfying, and you want out.

There is no room inside one's comfortable rut for children. They climb up and tear down its walls, flood it with apple juice and urine, tunnel through to accost strangers and enter your heart, and disrupt forever any sense of quiet tranquility it may have once provided. And ain't that just grand? It sure is for this prime time dad.

Do not misunderstand me. I am not saying one should have children to add zest to one's life. That level of selfishness is not conducive to raising kids or to a happy family life.

Back in those childless days of yesteryear, I thought of children mostly in terms of added responsibilities, burdens, and hardships. I was pleasantly surprised by the spice that our children added to my life. Their arrival helped me appreciate the distinct contrast between my life before kids and after, a difference akin to watching the game from the bleachers or being a starter on the team.

There's nothing like a change of view and a new roommate or two to open up your world and give you a new lease on life. The world outside of your familiar rut may be a bit scary at first, but you'll be fully alive, all senses attuned to a new, thriving life of spontaneous adventure and fresh opportunities.

The fire burning the retreat bridges to my old rut illuminates my new life's landscape. My children tug at my hands, leading me forward into our shared futures. Gently, kids, my basketball-jammed knuckles aren't what they used to be.

- - - - - - - - - - - - - - -

When venturing outside of your rut, remember to stretch. Stretching your muscles provides a limbering warm-up to help you attain goals in your physical life. The same is true for your psychological life.

When younger, you probably stretched far and wide to reach your ambitions. Nowadays, you may find yourself comfortable and complacent with your achievements. Stretching may seem too challenging, not worth the effort, a strenuous activity with too little return. But stretching yourself, discovering new horizons, is the essence of maintaining an intriguing life.

Sure, midlife fatherhood is a stretch, but it will help to keep you active, aware, in learning mode, and young. The demands on time, body, mind and spirit are substantial. But so are the rewards.

Decades ago I served as a press secretary for the 1976 Jimmy Carter Presidential Campaign. I traveled from state primary to state primary, sleeping on sofas, living on little (the joke was, all the peanuts we could eat), while Carter's candidacy picked up steam. After we won the nomination and the election, I worked in the Interior Department and on Capitol Hill. Politics was exciting, rewarding, it meant something, and I loved it.

But I left D.C. behind to help make a low budget horror movie, and after that, moved to California and began working for high technology companies in Silicon Valley. Sure, I'd get the phone calls from political buddies every presidential campaign season, and I almost went back on the campaign trail for a couple of candidates, but after awhile, a new crowd moved into the mainstream and political old timers like me get contacted mostly for monetary contributions.

When I worked in Washington, many of the political pros would lament the political scene back in home districts where their constituencies actually lived and voted. They warned that politics on the local level got too messy, too nasty, and often pitted neighbors against neighbors. Better to stay in Washington, where a level of abstraction over program and budgetary issues provided a buffering safety zone from the rough and tumble, hot-blooded interaction of opposing feet on the street.

And so, I stayed away from politics for twenty years. Then I had children, and began to understand and appreciate how the local schools worked.

Our unified public school district needed a parcel tax measure to support teachers and reduce class sizes, so I volunteered to be the campaign press secretary. I was doing it for my kids and children and families throughout the district.

We won that election by a big margin, and I was thrust into a world of ongoing local public policy debate, campaigning for city council and school board candidates, and volunteering for worthy organizations, in short, local politics.

Having children spurred me to become involved in activities that I thought I'd left behind. I find this reunion with my past passions thoroughly rewarding. I enjoy the heck out it.

Becoming a prime time dad got me up and out of my rut, and stretched me into a more fulfilling life. I'm convinced that the mature man who stretches his life to include children vastly enriches his own existence. Stretching into prime time fatherhood will not break you. It may make you.

....

THIRTY-SEVEN

YOU NOW CARE EVEN LESS ABOUT WHAT OTHERS THINK

As we mature and live through more of the vacillating vagaries of life, our personal, internally-muttered mantra increasingly shifts from "What will they think?" to "Frankly, my dear, I don't give a damn."

This healthy lack of concern about what others may or may not think about us helps build a positive psychological environment in which to raise children.

As a prime time dad, you will, of course, have self-doubts about your fathering skills. But the truth is that every dad, no matter his age, has self-doubts. It's normal. A beneficial aspect of your grown-up outlook is that you'll be less apt to allow your doubts and fears to run your life.

While there's much parenting help out there, there's also much hype. There's a beguiling assortment of children's products, programs, and theories purporting to boost IQs, learn during sleep, start to read, stop pooping in pull-ups, and get into an Ivy League school, all before the age of four.

In fact, it starts in utero. We played classical music to both of our kids when they were still buns in the oven. (No violin virtuosos in this house as of yet.)

And the peer pressure is enormous. Sometimes it seems that every mom and dad has a mandate to voice their particular (and often peculiar) convictions about every aspect of child rearing at every opportunity.

Whether they obtained their information through personal experience, a quick Google search, or Cousin Delbert's anecdotes makes no matter. The controversies abound and the advice goes dizzyingly round-and-round.

Both of our children attended a wonderful co-operative pre-school from before they were a year old through age four. Many of the parents at this school were rightfully concerned about nutrition, quality sustenance, food allergies, and the like. Let's just say, if the kids ever had a food fight, it would be organics only.

As a guy who grew up on cheeseburgers, fries, and Coca-Cola, I was a fish out of water, an Alice Cooper in an Alice Waters world. While other parents picnicked on kale-infused Greek yogurt, I took my son to Denny's.

We always sat at the counter. He could barely reach his food, but we sure had fun sitting side by side, twirling on our stools, watching our milkshakes get topped with whipped cream, doing tricks with the straws, and bantering with the wait staff. I wanted him to have that counter experience before it completely disappeared from our neck of the woods.

Back at the pre-school, I was a bit reluctant to discuss our Fonzi approach to lunch. But word got out, and rather than tsk-tsk frowns, I was surprised to receive slaps on the back and good-natured encouragement. Chalk up another minor victory for going your own way.

As a more mature man, you'll not be so swayed by the zeal of the spiel. You'll do your homework, consult the experts, then make decisions and stick with them unless and until the evidence of the results persuades you otherwise. You will not make child-rearing choices based upon what your uncle or your first wife or your church deacon or your barber thinks. After years of hearing the empty hot air of blustering bloviaries, you're well equipped to listen to and heed your own counsel.

This ability to pick a course and stick to it despite dissent's distractions helps you set limits, provides consistency and clarity, and establishes a sense of order and safety. These are all characteristics of a healthy environment in which to raise and nurture kids. You do give a damn, just not about all the petty prattle.

Section V.

In the Zone

THIRTY-EIGHT

....

REINTRODUCE
YOURSELF TO YOURSELF

As we grow up, we tend to grow apart from ourselves. We discard childish ways, drift from the past, aspire to new heights, bury bad memories, edit personal history, and strive for success, love, happiness, and a full life.

Life is a tangled web we weave, even if we do not practice to deceive. But I maintain that there resides in the core of us all an essential pure self who is good, a bit bewildered, and increasingly estranged as the years pass.

When I became a dad, I was re-introduced to this former self. I caught forgotten glimpses of me at an earlier age reflected in the antics and actions of my children. For example, my magical anticipation of Santa Claus' visit, the pride I had for my father, the safety and love I felt in my mother's arms. I marvel and smile at these reverie memories my children unwittingly ignite.

As these flashbacks would strike, I was amazed to realize how far I'd traveled away from the former me. The process of reconnecting, reuniting with myself was healing, like reaching back through time to shake hands and get reacquainted with a dear friend I hadn't thought about in years.

Many people dread high school class reunions. They feel they haven't achieved enough, have lost too much hair, or gained too much weight, or they can't face former mentors and tormentors.

But the people with whom I've discussed this issue invariably say they loved reconnecting with their former classmates. They talk about feeling those deep roots again, about filling gaps in their lives, achieving greater understanding, and becoming more whole.

My son was about one-year old when I turned the big 5-0, and I'd been experiencing this reconnection with the former me since we were expecting his arrival. I decided to throw a milestone party for myself, but what mattered most was inviting six of my childhood friends with whom I'd grown up but had lost touch.

These were my home boyz, some of them friends since before kindergarten. We'd gone through ups and downs, chats and spats, births and deaths, but we hadn't all been together in one spot at the same time for decades.

I got on the phone to begin the labyrinthian lobbying effort of convincing them to jet west for a weekend. One said yes, and I leveraged this commitment with others. To my surprise, eventually, they all agreed to join the reunion, our own unique version of *The Big Chill*. The weekend was such a hit that we've reconvened as a group in different parts of North America every few years since.

When I became a dad, I took a vivid trip through, and reunited with, a familiar personal landscape I'd forgotten about. I've found it is a most pleasant journey, full of surprises and insights. And yes, this reconnection with self is healing.

I'm not motivated or evolved enough to "work through" all of my "past issues." I'm quite content to watch them spontaneously unfold and transport me back to my earlier self in amusing, random, and enriching fashion. It's added extra texture to my life, and is another positive aspect of prime time parenthood I simply could not have predicted.

- - - - - - - - - - - - - -

Here's a parental posting on friendship for my children. Our children are beginning to encounter the tricky and treacherous turmoil of relationship trauma. Their friends can change allegiances and alliances, coveted party invitations may not arrive, choices must be made on whom to invite for special events, there's unhappiness with Mom and Dad's recommendations, and there are plenty of "he said, she said" tears shed.

You get the picture. Sensitive souls are trying to make sense of their own and others' not-always-considerate actions. Kinda like all of us at any age, isn't it?

I pondered how to help guide my children through this emerging minefield while flying home from a gathering of those old childhood pals. We met in Cleveland for a Buffalo Bills vs. Browns football game, jetting and driving in from all over the country. We hadn't gathered for many years, and since cold Great Lakes rain pelted us throughout the game, we really felt "the big chill."

In the air on the return flight, it hit me like the sunburst above the cloud layer over Cleveland. The lessons I've learned over the decades from my relationships with these boyhood buddies might just help my kids as they navigate the bumpy and bruising paths of friendships.

Now, I know passing along advice is not as easy as passing on genes or bad habits, but here's what I'm telling my children about Best Friends Forever (BFFs).

When in Doubt, Be Yourself

You are not what you think others think of you. You are a unique, wondrous individual with your own mind and your own ideas about how to spend your energies on this planet. Friends are important, but they are not as important as being true to yourself —being your own best friend— treating yourself with healthy respect. It doesn't matter a hoot what your friends say when you make your own determination that certain actions are not for you. You do not have to step on the gas, chugalug, hit the bong or bang the gong just because your posse pack pressures you. Go your own way. Do what you know is right for you. Good friends will reveal themselves when you're on your own correct journey, your sacred path. You are worthy of good friends. You are worthy of love. Nothing any silly bunch of immature fools might do or say can take that away from you.

The Wheel Turns – and Churns Back Around

Our gang of buddies was scattered to the winds for decades. People and circumstances change. Everyone pursues their own self-interests. It's natural for friends to grow estranged as they seek their own adventures, develop new skills and discover new pals. But months and even years later, you may find yourselves on the same sports team, partnering on a school project or intrigued by the same music, math or Matisse. Changes can swing you far away from close friends, and later, swing you right back together. You must learn to allow friends, and yourself, to change. Change is natural. Embrace it. Give everyone their space to grow.

Forgive, Forget, Forge Forward

We get hurt by, and hurt, those closest to us. Ancients, such as the Everly Brothers, taught us that everyone gets made blue and lied to, turned down and pushed 'round, cheated and mistreated. It's the way of the world. Misunderstandings are magnified among close friends. Perhaps the insult you think you heard was not really meant that way. Give your friends the benefit of the doubt. Practice biting your own tongue instead of using it to criticize. It's taken years, but our *Return of the Secaucus 7* gang seems finally ready to let old wounds heal and not pick at the scabs. Roll with the punches and hesitate to throw your own. Remember the wise saying: "Holding a grudge is like drinking poison and waiting for the other person to die." And as you trek forward toward your own goals and dreams, you may look over to find a friend's smiling face marching in the same direction right beside you.

Never Give Up on Your Friends

If you want a friend, be a friend. Support your pals, even as they grow out of your life. Don't write them off. Stay in touch. You may never know what hidden factors might be influencing their behavior. Keep reaching out to them. Some will pleasantly surprise you. Our gang of comrades had many

· more reunion invitation ideas rejected than accepted. But if we'd stopped after the first 10 failures, we'd never have gotten the opportunity to get soaked to the skin together in nose bleed seats at Cleveland Stadium. Okay, that may not be the best example, but you get the notion. Shared history is never forgotten, and the friends you now have may be the same ones who'll reach out to you when you're alone at a school dance, who'll lend a sympathetic ear to your silent scream for understanding, or who'll warn you of a dead end down the road. Don't give up on your buddies, and you might even see some of them when you reach my fossilized age, with impressions of lifelong friendships deeply embedded into your heart.

THIRTY-NINE

....

TRULY EXPAND YOUR CONSCIOUSNESS

Even if you're a young pup, you surely know something, some history, some stylized Hollywood flashback about the mind-expanding craziness of the 1960s and 1970s. What a long strange trip it was, from revolutionary ways of exploring personal and spiritual perceptions to radical self-empowerment political change to evolutionary initiatives in the environment and personal technological landscape.

Even though Timothy Leary really is dead now, there are still good, good, good, good vibrations humming in the universe, and you don't need mushrooms or Moonies or the Moody Blues to expand your consciousness.

Just have a kid. You will be rocketed into a new dimension the moment you see those shining eyes searching for and connecting with yours.

You will see the beauty, mystery, determination, and fragility of life wrapped up like a burrito. Behold the essence of human existence, as powerfully poignant today as in antiquity, squealing for a meal, a change, a nap, a human touch.

You will gain new insight and appreciation for your familial lineage, all of human history, and the hidden future. You will step outside of yourself, gain greater empathy and awareness, and by common bonds become more of a human being.

You need not be a psychedelic relic or lick a toad at Burning Man to raise your consciousness. Raise a child. Heck, the sleep deprivation alone will trigger an out of body experience.

FORTY

....

DISCOVER YOUR
PARALLEL UNIVERSE

Many moons ago, I swam for the first time in the crystal clear ocean waters of Maui. Scores of others nearby were diving with goggles, facemasks, and snorkels, spending most of their time down below, exploring the undersea world.

Being a veteran swimmer and body surfer where the Atlantic and Pacific Oceans touch our U.S. coastlines, I chuckled to myself, thinking how foolish they were. I could clearly see, even without a mask, that there was not much down there to look at. Must have been the first time those rubes saw the sandy ocean floor.

But then someone offered me a mask. I dove to discover an abundant, swirling world of multicolored aquatic life and action that had been invisible to my unprotected eye. I was astounded by the existence of both this undersea cavalcade and by my earlier arrogant ignorance.

Parenthood has given me a facemask to see an entirely new dimension to the world I thought existed. Forget hyperspace's superstring theory with its promise of eleven (or more) different dimensions. By becoming a prime time dad, I've discovered my parallel universe.

Nowadays, I don't just see a bunch of kids walking to school. I see each and every one of them in my parallel universe walking hand-in-hand with a legion of folks dedicated to ensuring their safe march to beat the bell.

I see their deeply populated world of parents packing lunches, doctors checking ears, teachers listening attentively to each sound as they read, the school district paying for crossing guards, grandparents picking them up after school, sport coaches, scout leaders, religious guides, elected officials, and all of them are huddled around the kids, protecting them, guiding them, inspiring them forward.

I cannot look at a dad today without seeing him holding his coughing, feverish child in his arms as they both pass out asleep in front of the television at 4:00 a.m. I now see his anxious efforts to ensure the family has enough money and meat, his persistent battle against household dangers, his patience during the endless hours spent hitting balloons back and forth to promote eye-hand coordination, and the thrill of his child's first base hit.

There exists in your community, wherever you live and right in front of you, an astonishingly sophisticated parallel universe of parent- and child-oriented services and activities that is thriving and vibrating with the deepest of meaning.

Before becoming a later life dad, I paid little, if any attention to this "kid world." Why would I? It was simply not on my radar screen.

But I've discovered by wearing my fatherhood facemask that this parallel universe of child-centric action is indeed the very heart and soul of my community. By becoming a prime time dad, I've rocketed out of my comfortable reality and into an exciting parallel universe, and the hyperspace is just fine, thank you.

FORTY-ONE

....

SLOW DOWN THE
ACCELERATION OF TIME

As we mature, we become increasingly aware that time flies. We speed through the years at an accelerating rate. Remember those languorous summers of youth? Now it's practically Labor Day before you get to a double header. Life can move too fast for us to consciously acknowledge it, let alone appreciate and enjoy it.

But there is a way to slow down this relentless, inevitable speeding up of time. Have kids, and you'll discover what I call my parental paradox of time.

It's really about the duality of time spent with children. Sure, one day you're feeding them baby food, and it seems like the next day you're shelling out more money so they can buy their own popcorn or iPhone. Long stretches of time still whiz by.

But if you really focus on those moments when you teach your child how to put on underwear, tie a shoe, build a soon-to-be-toppled tower of blocks, hear the difference in pronunciation between "three" and "sree," find animals in cloud patterns, or how subtraction can be checked by addition, time stands wondrously still.

You enter into a bubble outside of normal time, a space where the creative connections made with your children transcend everyday reality. It's the artist's melting clock landscape of intense higher inspiration and consciousness. And it is joyful.

On the other hand, the parental paradox of time is not always friendly. Time stops and sluggish seconds plod agonizingly forward in slowest motion when you're bent over, back aching, unsuccessfully trying to strap your squirming youngster into a car seat designed by de Sade.

The worst time paradox happens when you completely lose your mind and allow yourself, against all previous experience, to harbor any expectations that things may actually go the way you anticipated.

For example, say you've made sure your children completed all their homework before feeding them and carting one to a Cub Scout meeting and the other to swim practice.

Back home, safe and sound, you give each a spelling test to prep them for the next school day, and allow them to play with a bit of electronics or watch some television before they go to night-night land, that golden hour when you anticipate watching a missed movie in your high def den.

Bedtime approaches. Tick, tick, tock. It's coming, you're savoring it. It's soon to be Daddy's time. You've done everything, the wife who's at her meeting will owe you so big time, you're proud of yourself, and that movie's supposed to be great.

"Okay, kids, time to brush teeth and get to bed." But they want to read. They want a glass of milk. They want a snack. They want to discuss their day, sleep with Dad, prepare the Yugioh deck for the next day's battle, double-check their homework, take a shower, and the list goes on and on.

You'd think that pouring a plastic glass of milk and getting a bowl of cereal might take about one minute or so. But when moving through the molasses of the parental paradox of time, especially with that foolish overlay of anticipating the end of the day's duty and fun free time ahead, every moment slogs through a hibernation of immobility.

Your blood pressure rises, your heart races, you try to be civil, but like the dream where you make no progress running away from monsters, the harder you try, the less progress you make.

Segments of parental life slow down and linger. Sometimes they're poetically rewarding, sometimes maddeningly interminable, but they will unfold every day in myriad ways.

Look for them, enter into them, be there now with them, and you can slow down and stretch the mindless rush into a series of meaningful moments suspended from time's relentless advance.

FORTY-TWO

....

YOU'LL STAY MARRIED
AND LIVE LONGER

S tatistical studies show that married men live longer than single men. I guess stretching out their exposure to us is just another one of the charming ways we make our spouses deliriously happy.

But seriously, men do live longer in stable, committed relationships, and it is my contention that your spousal connection is deepened, strengthened, and metaphysically melded when you share the adventures of parenthood.

You'll never feel closer to another human being than after holding your spouse's leg to her belly as she pants and pushes your baby out and into breathing life (or, go through the adoption, family blending, alternative insemination, or whatever baby-producing process is in your tea leaves).

Yes, there are difficulties to be overcome in parenthood. Differing opinions, arguments over duties, exhausted communications, disruption of routines, and the like all contribute to the list of problems to be surmounted.

But, this life in the foxhole, this battle to do the right thing, this naturally forced teamwork you will share with your spouse builds bonds and connections that transcend the richness of your childless relationship.

Raising your children is a collaborative effort of the highest order. The worthiness of the goal and the energy required right-sizes many disagreements to a more trivial status.

Most things get demoted to a place where they're just not worth the time and effort to argue about. And if you're tempted toward a tempest, first look around the house. Your son is detaching the bag from the overflowing vacuum cleaner and your daughter is using your carpet as a canvas.

You will be forged into a tight team dedicated to the survival of your children and yourselves. You will wildly waltz to the kiddie two-step with your spouse until you drop, then wake up, hear that baby drumbeat, and dance some more. You and your wife will strategize and muddle through new plays daily as you run a hurry-up offense with no time to huddle.

In our house, duties are informally delegated. For example, Lucy is the lead swim mom, helping our daughter with all her swim team practices, gear, and meets. I'm the basketball dad for our son, providing tips and one-on-one practice when he allows, sweating every contest from the stands, keeping stats for the coach, and driving to the many games and practices for his school, NJB, and AAU leagues.

Lucy's a better cook than I, so she puts the meals together. I do the bills and the money management. Lucy essentially takes care of inside the house while I take care of outside the house, yard work, and vehicles. She runs the washing machine, I fold the laundry. You get the picture.

While we have this division of labor, it came about naturally, based on our preferences and abilities. If someone slacks off on their end of the unspoken bargain, the other helps out. Or the slacker is made keenly aware of the discrepancy. I'm doing many more dishes nowadays.

You'll grow to rely upon, appreciate, and trust your wife in new, deeper, and varied ways. And as you intertwine your parental lives, you'll together weave a unique, personal, multi-textured familial tapestry.

Through the give and take, sharing, and compromising of the intensive parenting process, you will sharpen your shared vision, establish and work toward common goals, love more thoroughly, strengthen your marriage, and thus, live a longer life.

Oh, you lucky, lucky ladies.

Section VI.

Pushing Forward
the Finish Line

FORTY-THREE

....

HAVING KIDS WILL KEEP
YOU YOUNG

I often tell people that my children will either keep me young or put me in an early grave, and that the jury is still out. It's good for a chuckle, but the truth is, I'm increasingly convinced that having kids is indeed keeping me young.

Midlife dads can benefit enormously from raising children. They keep you physically active, they keep your mind alert and in learning mode, they keep you centered in the present, truly humble, connected to family, friends, and community, and they help you stay playfully youthful in heart and spirit.

How can one stay grumpy and worried about family finances while watching your kindergartener's class sing "Over the river and through the woods" at the annual Thanksgiving Day performance? After dinner, kids need a horsy ride or a game of Crazy Eights more than Dad needs another dose of the world's bad news.

Awhile back, my then 10-year-old son practiced a few notes on the trombone, and had my wife and me in hysterics. He valiantly struggled to hold this rather large instrument, almost the size of him, while blowing flatulent-sounding vibrations that rattled the windows throughout the neighborhood.

Mirthful tears flowed from my eyes as I remembered that what seemed like just yesterday he was making the same sounds in his diaper. If laughter is the best medicine, kids are plentiful dispensers.

I'm the grateful beneficiary of my kids' smorgasbord of interests and activities. My son now plays me one-on-one basketball, and my daughter races me in the swim team pool. The exercise, camaraderie, and the range of new experiences add healthful joy and zest, and I'm betting, longevity to my life.

The kids help keep me active and alert. I'm trying to add up the new math, re-learning basketball offense strategies, analyzing anti-bullying techniques, contributing to PTA and school district causes, and constantly going to new places, events, and activities rather than sitting on the couch watching television.

As a prime time dad, I have first-hand knowledge of the inevitable fade of youth. It's not an abstract concept off somewhere in the future. I know the hour glass sand slips through our fingers. So I grasp the moments before they fall away.

We all have choices in our daily lives about how much to get involved, how much energy to expend, how much to give and live. My children help me choose to get up and out and on with it. Being present in their lives provides me with countless ways to recover a youthful vitality.

I've found fatigue to be more of a mental state than a physical one. Invariably when I groan and grouse that I must leave my easy chair for a Cub Scout meeting or a student play rehearsal, I find myself energized at the functions.

When I discuss staying young, I'm not talking about my outsides. I'm not getting a hairpiece or a face lift or liposucked or a hot red sports car. This is an inside job. I feel younger because the old me is evolving into an improved me who tries to see the world a bit more through my children's fresh eyes.

I'm adapting, changing, breaking through boundaries, and rethinking what's possible. All of this, and more, is keeping me young. And it's coming at the perfect time for me. Youth is wasted on the young. They're incapable of appreciating it. The prime time dad truly can.

....

FORTY-FOUR

JOIN THE WORLD'S LARGEST FRATERNITY

E agerly entering a party back when I was single and childless, I remember being dismayed to find that the hosts had also invited some of their fellow parents, who brought their children in tow. I knew immediately that this was not going to be the kind of raucous, raise the roof party I'd anticipated.

The parents all gathered on the floor in a big collegial circle, kids stumbling everywhere, parents gabbing on and on with each other about pabulum and poop, showing off baby photos, and all of them absolutely oblivious to the rest of us.

What was wrong with those parents? Weren't they interested in the splendid opinions about the latest movie or restaurant or technology we non-parents discussed? How could they come dressed like that to a party, in sweatpants and slobber-stained shirts, with sticky goo, probably puke, in their hair? And why weren't they drinking, letting loose, and striking for sparks to burn down the house like the rest of us?

I never forgot that party. The parents sat on the floor, changing diapers, wiping spit, making sure their kids were not stepped upon, and engaging deeply in conversations about, what else, their kids and parenting. They could not have cared less about the shenanigans the rest of us childless ones were performing. They were having a great time. I wasn't.

It was not until I became a dad that this made sense to me. When you have a child, you enter into the world's largest fraternity. There's no pledging, no secret handshake or song or rituals to join Delta Phi Parenthood. (There will be Hell Nights, but you won't be blindfolded.)

You'll know your brothers and sisters by the understanding looks they give you when your child emits an ear piercing scream in a reserved restaurant. They will help you open your jogging stroller when your arms are filled with diaper bags, baby bottles, and a Baby Bjorn.

You can talk to any of them, with sincere communicative interest, on just about any subject dealing with parenthood. And this conversation goes on through pre-school and elementary school, sports programs, music lessons, you name it.

You'll learn tricks and techniques, share stories, reject bad advice, admit your most personal fears and failures, and feel elated that so many of your fellow human beings walking on the planet understand what you're going through, and want to help. I am truly grateful that my becoming a dad has allowed me admission into the club at the very heart of humanity: Parenthood.

- - - - - - - - - - - - - - -

And I'm now running with some famous jet setters and celebrities. According to information gathered from Internet sources, here are some famous men and their later life dad ages: David Bowie (at 53), Mick Jagger (at 57), Michael Douglas (at 58), Rod Stewart (at 60), Paul McCartney (at 61), Eric Clapton (at 59), Pierre Trudeau (72), Charlie Chaplin (at 73), Saul Bellow (at 84), Pablo Picasso (at 68), David Letterman (at 56), Larry King (at 65 and 66),

Woody Allen (at 51), Warren Beatty (at 62), Dennis Quaid (at 50), Jack Nicholson (at 53), Steve Martin (at 67), and Tom Arnold (at 54).

Joining the fraternity of fatherhood will not exactly have you running with a list of the rich and famous, but you will be running just like them, one foot at a time, aching back bent, breathlessly chasing your toddler, who's trying to run up a down escalator. But hey, that's show biz!

FORTY-FIVE

....

THERE'S A PROFOUND NEED FOR FATHERS

As mature men who mean what we say, I maintain that if you decide to become a father, you'll stick around to do the job right, no matter what. Children benefit from dads. Research clearly suggests that fatherless children are more susceptible to drug and alcohol abuse, teen pregnancy, criminal behavior and even jail time. Society needs the gentle strength and firm love of fathers.

If traditional or step-fatherhood is not an option, you may want to consider the many possibilities available to serve as a surrogate dad to those who would gladly lay down the welcome mat.

As a wiser, mature, midlife man, you have considerable qualifications to enrich the lives of children in need. Society screams out for you. Should you decide to fill the void, you will no doubt fulfill your life.

While the majority of American children are born to fathers between the ages of 20 and 34, becoming a prime time dad is a distinct national trend. Increasingly, you'll have plenty of company. The growing numbers of prime time dads don't match those of the hoola-hoop or the pet rock or the latest iPortable sales, but they do underscore that many midlife men are now taking stock of their lives and finding new meaning and life fulfillment by raising children. Prime time dads are not statistical anomalies and sideshows. They're trendsetters.

Along with this trend are many reports about the potential negative aspects of fathering children later in life. Studies indicate that children of older dads may face increased chances of ailments such as autism, schizophrenia, and some forms of cancer.

I am not a doctor, and I cannot properly evaluate or advise on these important topics. There are risks. There are risks associated with everything in nature. Conception does not guarantee perfection.

Each family must consider the risks and rewards for themselves and make their own decisions. I urge everyone to gain as much knowledge as possible before proceeding with parenthood in midlife or at any age.

This book is about my own life-enhancing experience, and I can only speak for me and my family. Our children are normal, healthy, and thriving. And their addition to my life has transformed me into a more normal, healthy, and thriving human being.

Sure, it can get more like Ozzy Osbourne than Ozzie and Harriet around our house. It's no pocket full of posies, and midlife fatherhood is not for everyone. I was truly afraid to become a dad in my late 40s. Like Dante entering Hades, I was almost resigned to abandon all hope. Instead, it's turned out to be the best thing I've ever done.

If you're a mature man thinking about becoming a father, I want you to know that I was genuinely surprised and deeply enriched by the rewarding nature of prime time fatherhood. I was astonished by the advantages I have parenting as a more mature man, and thunderstruck by my profound, positive, personal metamorphosis.

CONCLUDING REMARKS

....

This book presents primarily positive views and anecdotes about later-blooming fatherhood. After all, that's the book's vision, its strategic construction. It's about 45 reasons to embrace midlife fatherhood, not reasons to reject it.

Naturally, the concepts and stories conveyed herein do not cover the entirety of my daddy journey. This is not a full-fledged parental memoir. Some of the fears and jeers and tears I've experienced simply don't fit the book's point of view. But honestly, the positives far out-number the negatives, exponentially so.

Becoming a prime time dad led me to a unique consciousness that transforms negatives into positives. For example, I thought running around after a poopy toddler would tire me. In fact, these chores help keep me in shape and prod me toward better food and fitness.

I thought younger parents would exclude me because I was older. But I learned parenthood is the great equalizer, and it's brought me closer to other moms and dads, whatever their ages, because most of us realize we're all in this together.

I figured I would not have the energy for Boy Scouts and Little League and swim team and school plays. The truth is, these outings have become energizing joys that enrich my life in ever surprising textural twists and turns.

Frankly, what I thought about later blooming fatherhood before I became a dad was mostly wrong. It's a good thing I did not act solely on my fears. I hope to have set the record straighter with this book.

Now that you know how well qualified you are to be a prime time dad, remember that it will test every aspect of your physical, psychological, and spiritual self. But diamonds are created from pressure and pearls from irritation. Great fathers are works in progress. You have all the raw materials for shining success. Just add courage, compassion, commitment, and some baby vomit.

Here's to healthy, thriving children, families, and prime time dads.

ACKNOWLEDGMENTS

....

Developing and living an attitude of gratitude is a life-enhancing, and in my case, life preserving exercise I try to perform on a daily basis.

I am grateful first of all to my wife, Lucy, whose love and devotion to our family inspires and awes me. She skillfully reads multiple drafts of all my writings, even though I suspect she sometimes considers the editing drudgery as unpleasant a necessity as was changing diapers.

I am grateful to my publisher, Michele Gibson of Bright Lights Press (www.brightlightspress.com), who enthusiastically supported me through rewrites and word fights, first rights and technical bytes.

I am grateful to my childhood chum Don Loy. He's read and critiqued my various writings over the years, and he's always found an agreeable way to disagree.

I am grateful to those who provided me cover quotes and additional information on the important issue of midlife fatherhood: David Carnoy, Larry King, Frank LaLoggia, Tom Parker, Victor Thomas, Adriana Trigiani, Kristi Walsh, and David Zeiger.

I am grateful to Kris Loew (www.loewco.com) for her upbeat cover design artistry, and to Lisa Noble (www.lisanoblephotography.com) and Gordon McIver (www.rebelsun.com) for their photographic expertise.

I am grateful to Bud and Ling Genovese, whose enterprising support has helped keep this craft on course.

And lastingly, I am grateful to my children for leading me on this truly transcendent journey to the center of the heart.

ABOUT THE AUTHOR

Photo by Lisa Noble

Len Filppu is a writer/screenwriter who's worked as a communications executive in Silicon Valley, served as a press secretary to Jimmy Carter and on Capitol Hill, and helped produce a low budget rock 'n' roll horror movie. The best thing he ever did was to become a first-time father in midlife.

Visit www.primetimedads.com to connect with Len, and to read about and share with others the adventures of prime time fatherhood.

Read Len's *Huffington Post Parents* columns at http://www.huffingtonpost.com/len-filppu, and follow him at: www.twitter.com/MidlifeDad.